The Islands
Of The
Argosaronic Gulf

Betty Kagia

The Islands of the Argosaronic Gulf

Salamina
Aigina - Angistri - Methana
Poros (Galatas, Trizina)
Hydra - Spetses

Grecocard Publications
Athens 1995

Editor: George Monemvassitis
General Text Supervision: Betty Kagia
Photography: Kostas Xenikakis, Loukas Hapsis, Pantelis Voukouris
Translation: Marian Grozou
Colour Separation: Fotokitaro Ltd.
Maps and Plans: SI Advertising
Printing and Binding: S. Nanos & Co. S.A.
ISBN: 960-7436-06-7

Dear readers,

As you will discover on reading this book, I have attempted to compile under one cover written records of history and folklore in combination with data gleaned from oral tradition. I have also attempted, without sacrificing scientific accuracy on basic historical and social points, to create pleasant but informative reading matter for islanders and visitors alike. During my few days' stay on the islands, I tried to collect as much information as possible. I completed my research in Athens, always with the help of islander friends, who have stood by me all this time. I hope that experts will view my efforts favourably. I would also like to stress that in spite of my honest endeavours and my love for the islands, unintentional errors or omissions may have occurred: with your help they can be avoided in future editions. I would also like to stress that the reader who wishes to learn more about the historical events that took place in the Argosaronic Gulf should read the general history of the area, which is more analytical and detailed.

I feel the obligation to make it clear that this book would never have come about without the help of the islanders, eponymous and anonymous, who by contributing invaluable information have filled these pages with their knowledge and love of the islands. In particular I would like to thank the following people: From Salamina, Maria Boutsi, employee of the Municipality's Cultural Department; Anna Lalanga, head of the Municipality's Cultural Department; Demetrios Pallas, Professor Emeritus of Byzantine Archaeology at Athens University; Evgenia Perdikouri, employee of the Salamina Archaeological Museum; Vassilios Papanikolaou, Chairman of the Society for Culture and the Improvement of the Environment "Euripides". From Aigina, Ekaterini Thanopoulou, librarian; Georgia Koulikourdi, historian; Georgios Kalokentis, employee of Aegina Municipality; Evi Touloupa, former Chief Curator of the Acropolis; Georgios Bakomitros, tourist agency owner; Trifonas Gotzis, Mayor of Aigina. From Angistri, Vassilios Anastassiou, Secretary of Angistri Municipality. From Methana, Dimitris Kondogiannis, merchant; Sotirios Stathakis, Mayor of Methana; Kiriaki Skourti, Municipality Secretary. From Poros, Georgios Athanassiou, Vice-Chairman of the Library; Spiros Spiridon, Mayor of Poros; Sakis Papamitrou, Assistant Mayor of Poros. From Galatas, Athanassia Danopoulou, Commune employee. From Trizina, Panagiotis Sarandopoulos, Commune Secretary. From Hydra, Konstantinos Stroumboulis, Assistant Mayor of Hydra; Konstantina Adamopoulou-Pavlou, Director of the Historical Archives. From Spetses, Georgios Thimaras, Mayor of Spetses; Georgios Stamatiou, philologist.

Betty Kagia

Contents

Out of Europe's 400 or so inhabited islands, six lie just a few miles from Athens. They are the small but beautiful islands of the Argosaronic (Argolic and Saronic) Gulf. Close by the port of Piraeus is the historic island of Salamina (ancient Salamis); just to the south Aigina, renowned for its ancient temples and medieval town; behind it Angistri, a small paradise; further down towards the Peloponnese Methana, famous for its healing springs and Poros, well-known for the Amphictyony which met in its temple of Poseidon. South of the Argolic peninsula lies Hydra and around to the west Spetses, islands boasting impressive sea-captains' mansions and powerful fleets which made history in the modern era.

Continuously inhabited since antiquity, their rich historical and cultural tradition, marvellous climate, myriad natural beauties, well-developed tourist infrastructure and, most importantly, their proximity to Attica make them popular vacation spots for Athenians as well as foreign visitors.

History of the Argosaronic Gulf Area

When the Greek land began to be formed 30 million years ago, most of the islands of the Aegean were connected to each other, except for those which were closest to the coast of the mainland and still formed part of it. The presence in the area of four great volcanoes (in Aegina, Methana, Poros and Milos) added to the geological upheavals. Certain other islands arose from the disintegration of mountain massifs through the action of torrential rains. Thus Poros, Spetses, Dokos and Spetsopoula were nothing more than an extension of the Argolic landmass.

During the latter part of the Palaeolithic Era, the level of the sea dropped down even lower, forming a coastal plain around the Argolid, connecting it to Hydra. A land bridge linked the Methana peninsula to Salamina and the southern coast of Attica. None of the islands of the Argosaronic Gulf show any signs of habitation from those times, with the exception of two flint arrowheads found in Zogeria on Spetses (probably evidence of a visit by hunters on foot seeking water, from the nearby Fraghthi Cave on the Argolic Gulf, where a form of primitive society flourished in Mesolithic times).

Nor is there any evidence of human habitation from the Neolithic Era, possibly because the level of the sea was rising constantly, destroying any means of communication with Fraghthi, the well-developed centre of habitation in Argolis. It was only in Aegina that colonists from the Peloponnese established settlements, on Kolona hill and in Messagros.

The islands of Hydra, Spetses and Spetsopoula took on their present-day form after the great earthquake of the 4th-3rd millennium BC, which brought about the destruction of most of the cave-settlements along with the coastal area of Argolis. Like any disaster, this one, too, was followed by an influx of settlers, Indo-Europeans who brought the use of bronze with them. As cultivation of the land and trade were developed, seaside settlements were created to facilitate navigation by a great new early Helladic centre, that of Lerna (2400-2100 BC). Thus, nineteen early Helladic settlements have been located in Aegina, Spetses, Hydra, Dokos and Velopoula (an islet between Spetses and Milos). They were used as way-stations between the Peloponnese and the Cyclades. These first inhabitants lived in peaceful communities and their chief occupations were shipping, fishing, obsidian-working, cultivating the land and herding sheep and goats.

Around 2100 BC, Lerna was destroyed and her island stations in the Argolic Gulf were abandoned, not to be settled again until the Myceneans had become masters of the seas. About the same time a new population factor, whose identity is unknown to us, made its appearance, arriving from the north. This Middle Helladic people settled Aegina and showed a preference for a closed agricultural economy. They used bronze weapons, as well as a new animal, the horse.

The dominant element in the population during Late Helladic times (13th century BC) was the mountain-dwelling Dryopians (inhabitants of what is now Thessaly), who appeared in Aegina, Hydra and Dokos. In Spetses and Poros their presence was very limited; it can be assigned to the end of the Late Helladic Era. When sea links later began to be forged again, the island's seaside settlements were used as mooring-places, havens and supply-depots for ships.

At the end of the 13th century BC, the islands took part in the 10-year Trojan War, Aegina making a greater contribu-

One of the area's four large volcanoes, the Methana volcano

9

Aegina and Salamis evolved into powerful religious, economic and commercial centres of Greece.

tion than the rest. Around the same time, a violent earthquake struck the whole Eastern Mediterranean basin, causing many springs to dry up; this had a disastrous effect on much of the farmland in the Argolid. In contrast, seaside towns and island ports were strengthened.

Around the end of the Mycenean Era (approximately 1170 BC), Aegina the great and powerful was attacked by the Myceneans; it remained sparsely populated for the next two hundred years, until the Dorian invasion. Almost all the island settlements in Hydra, Spetses and Dokos were also attacked. Not long after (1000 BC) Mycenean civilisation itself collapsed, when the Dorians, kinsmen of the Dryopians from the north, established themselves by force throughout the Peloponnese.

Because the islands have yielded no post-Mycenean finds, we may assume that they remained virtually uninhabited and obscure, with the exception of Aegina and Salamis, which developed into powerful Greek centres of economy and trade during the Archaic Age.

In the mid-7th century BC, the Amphictyony of Calauria appeared on the scene; established around the end of the 8th century, it was centred around the existing temple of Calaurian Poseidon on Poros. Members of this maritime, religious and political federation were the city-states of Athens, Aegina, Epidaurus, Hermione, Nauplia, Prasiae and Or-

chomenus, which joined forces in order to defend their independence and their commerce from the Argives. When the ruler of Argos seized Nauplia, he asked to join the Amphictyony. As finds from the sanctuary reveal, it then acquired great power and kept it until 459 BC. The Amphictyony began to lose its singular tribal character when Sparta occupied Prasiae and became a member. It continued to exist, however, until the 3rd century BC.

Early in the 5th century BC, when the Persian fleet sailed into the Aegean, none of the islands offered any resistance. Ten years after their defeat at Marathon, the Persians launched a second attack on Greece. Xerxes himself led the campaign, with Mardonius as his general. They set out in the spring of 480 BC from Sardis, capital of Lydia in Asia Minor, and after crossing the Hellespont began their invasion, conquering the city-states they encountered on their way with relative ease. The Greeks, united under Themistocles the Athenian and Thrasybulus the Spartan, mustered their naval forces in Salamis. These included contingents from Aegina, Corinth, Megara, Plataea and Thebes, and possibly Hydra and Spetses. On September 22nd of 480 BC, the fleets came together in battle, and Xerxes was routed. The Battle of Salamis was of major importance, not only for Greece but for the whole of Europe, because it checked the Persians' advance.

When the two most powerful Greek

city-states, Athens and Sparta, began to vie with each other for supremacy, the terrible Peloponnesian War began. It soon spread to encompass the Argosaronic area. In 425 BC the Athenian general Nikias seized Methana from Troezen (present-day Trizina) and garrisoned Athenian troops there, who plundered the surrounding areas. It would appear that the Athenians set up a network of seaside fortresses throughout the Argosaronic islands. The devastating civil war came to an end in 404 BC, with the overwhelming victory of Lysander the Spartan at Aigospotamoi, and commerce and shipping were resumed in the islands of the Argosaronic.

The growth of the city of Halieis (present-day Porto Heli) on the coast near Hermione – which received refugees from Tiryns during the 5th century, and had become a powerful and wealthy city-state by the 4th – was advantageous to Spetses, which would appear to have been a territorial extension of its dominion. Hydra belonged to Troezen, which used the island for grazing its herds.

In the middle of the 4th century a new power, the Macedonians, made their appearance in the Greek world; their objective was to bring about the national unity of Greece. When Philip II died and was succeeded by his son, Alexander the Great, the Greek city-states devoted themselves to peaceful works for a short time. The islands of the Argosaronic Gulf must have been a quiet backwater throughout this period, as the lack of archaeological finds would seem to indicate. The news of Alexander's death reawoke the Greek city-states, which reacted by trying to throw off the Macedonian yoke. Two Confederacies were then created in Greece, the Achaean and the Aetolian, but Alexander's successors quelled every attempt at rebellion. They even set up garrisons on the acropoles of the large city-states, granting them relative autonomy; thus, the islands of the Argosaronic Gulf were once again relegated to serving as naval bases or grazing land.

When the city of Halieis was razed by the Macedonian Demetrius the Besieger (303 BC), the rest of the Argosaronic islands slipped into obscurity along with it.

In 273 BC, the Methana volcano erupted for the last time, changing the morphology of the Gulf. Sphaeria was cut off from Methana; together with Calauria, it forms what is now Poros. Marshes came into being on the islands, forcing

Clay pots, figurines and a headless statue of a woman from the acropolis of Troezen, early 4th century (Poros Museum)

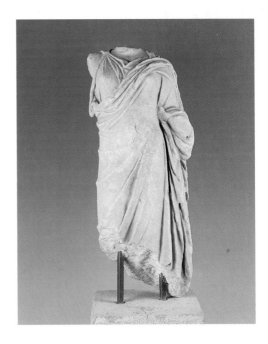

The temple of Calaurian Poseidon offered asylum to shipwrecked sailors and the persecuted. Demosthenes, the uncompromising Athenian orator, sought asylum here in 322 BC, when he was in danger of being arrested by Macedonian soldiers.

the islanders to move inland.

In Hellenistic times, the city of Methana was used by the Egyptians as a naval base from which they launched their attacks on the Macedonian garrisons in Spetses and Hydra.

When the Second Punic War came to an end in 202 BC, the Romans began casting about for a chance to get revenge on Philip V of Macedonia for having allied himself with the Carthaginian General Hannibal. Pretexts were soon found, but the underlying cause was none other than Rome's expansionist designs on Greece. In 167 BC, after repeated, long-drawn-out clashes with the Macedonians, the Romans took advantage of the internal discord among the Greek city-states, and conquered Greece, which became a Roman province. The forced peace brought about by the *Pax Romana* proved a boon to coastal navigation and the shipping trade in the Argosaronic Gulf, in turmoil up to that time.

This situation did not last long, however, as the Gulf was the target of repeated pirate raids. Early in the first century BC the ambitious king of Pontus, Mithridates VI, son of Eupator, allied himself with pirates from Cilicia and Crete and clashed with the Romans, inciting the Greeks to revolt. Mithridates was checked by the Roman Proconsul Leucius Cornelius Sulla in 86 BC. The Cilician pirates, after the defeat of their allies, began to plunder the coastal areas and the islands, destroying cities and temples, including Poseidon's in Calauria. The seaside areas were once again deserted and trade was carried on over land. This was why the geographer Strabo considered the Argosaronic islands unworthy of note. (His words are confirmed by the absence of any ruins or even isolated archaeological finds.)

In AD 396, the Visigoths, led by their king Alaric, raided and laid waste to most of the islands of the Argosaronic Gulf, along with a large portion of the Peloponnese: many refugees fled to Aegina. In the 9th century AD, Saracen pirates based on Crete ravaged the Aegean coasts, capturing and selling slaves.

When the Crusaders conquered Constantinople in 1204, they signed a treaty with the Venetians dividing up the Byzantine Empire. The islands came into Venetian hands, where they remained until 1460. (An exception was Aegina, which was not taken over by the Venetians until 1452.) The Venetian Admiral F. Morosini fortified most of the islands of the Argosaronic Gulf and used them as bases of operations against Turkish pirates.

After the Byzantine state submitted to the Turks, the islands suffered the brunt of the wars between Turkey and Venice. When the Turks became masters of the Peloponnese in 1470, they furiously persecuted the Greeks and Greek Orthodox Arvanites (Albanians, descendants of the ancient Illyrians) living there, who fled to the Argosaronic islands. The worst destruction was caused in October 1537 by the fearsome pirate and Admiral of the Turkish fleet, Khayr al-Din Barbarossa. The treaty of 1540 put an end to the Turco-Venetian War and the islands were conclusively signed over to the Turks. The devastated islands were resettled by Greek and Arvanite farmers and mercenary soldiers, chiefly from Nauplio and Monemvassia, in the wake of Turkish persecution in 1540.

But Russia had begun to foment rebellion against Greece's Turkish masters; following the reforms introduced by Peter the Great, she was ready to take her place among Europe's Great Powers. During the war between Russia and Turkey in 1768-1774, most of the islands took part in the Orloff events, including the revolt of the Peloponnese in 1768 and the attack of the Russian fleet on the Turks in 1770, for which they were mercilessly sacked by the Turks and Albanians. On July 1774 the Küçük Kaynarca Treaty, signed by the Russians and Turks, returned the islands to the latter.

Spetses and Hydra enjoyed a special form of government, whereby they were all but independent, self-administered by elders and Turkish deputies appointed by the islanders. In addition, both fleets gained the privilege of sailing, armed, under the protection of the Russian flag; thus they were ready to ward off pirate attacks, and their sailors became experienced in fighting naval battles. A period of economic development followed, fueled mainly by shipping and trade. It was fed even further by the outbreak of the Napoleonic Wars in 1797 and the blockade of Mediterranean ports by the English. The two fleets gained the monopoly in supplying foodstuffs to Italy, France and Spain, transporting wheat from the granaries of southern Russian and Romania. They ran the English blockade and exchanged their cargo for

The islanders have aptly named Palea Hora in Aegina "second Mistras". Cubical medieval houses clung amphitheatrically to the hillside all the way to the top; narrow, winding streets led to the town's 365 churches.

gold. The ship-owners (*nikokirei = "wealthy men"*) filled their coffers and built stately mansions which still stand as witnesses to the islands' great economic boom of those years.

In 1821 the Argosaronic Gulf became the centre of the Greek War of Independence and its islands were recorded in the most glorious pages of Greek history. The merchant navy was transformed into a revolutionary naval force. Hydra and Spetses played the role of a catalyst in waging and winning the Revolution. The experienced sailors and shipowners generously placed all their property at the disposal of the cause; it has been said, quite correctly, that it was won at sea. The sea-captains Kountouriotis, Tombazis, Voulgaris and Tsamados from Hydra, Bouboulina, Hatzigiannis Mexis and Barbatsis from Spetses, and Mathesis and Glistis

Hydra's Metropolis: the renowned marble altar-screen, the four chandeliers (The gilded one, in the style of Louis XIV, was stolen in 1792 from Les Tuileries and sold to the Hydraean sea-captain Sarkossis in 1812) and the brass candelabra are all gifts from the island's rich sea-captains, acquired on their travels.

from Salamis distinguished themselves for their bravery and patriotism. They joined the Friendly Society, a secret organisation established in Odessa, Russia, in 1816 to organise the armed struggle. The moment the Revolution was declared

The statue of the heroine Bouboulina in Possidonio Square in Spetses

on the islands, the ships began to fly the revolutionary flag. According to the Curator of the National Historical Museum, I. Metopoulos, its symbols were, with only slight variations, from island to island: a cross on a crescent moon, a snake wound round an anchor, a bird, and a spear.

These islands also played an important part after the Revolution, as they became the seats of the various provisional governments. The administrative committee of A. Zaimis installed itself in Aegina in 1826. Ioannis Kapodistrias, the Russian Foreign Minister from 1776 to 1831, was elected governor of Greece in the third National Assembly in Troezen in 1827. His government, recognised by the three Great Powers (England, France and Russia), established itself first in Aegina and then in Poros. Their ambassadors gathered in Poros in 1828 to meet with Kapodistrias to set the boundaries of the new Greek state. It was in Aegina in 1829 that the newly-formed state's first coin was minted.

During the 18th and 19th centuries, parts of ancient buildings were widely used as ready-made building materials or decorative elements in the construction of houses, churches and harbour works. Although during the post-revolutionary years steam and oil relegated the powerful shipowners and maritime towns to obscurity, and the centre of commercial and maritime activity shifted first to Syros and then to Piraeus, the old wooden sailing ships and the men who built them were not vanquished. Most islanders continued to earn their living in shipping, wooden ship-building and fishing.

On April 6, 1941, Hitler attacked Greece for the first time and united his forces with those of Italy. On June 11, 1943, the Italians surrendered to the Allies and on September 8th, the Germans took Rome. That same year saw the beginning of the German occupation in the Argosaronic Gulf. It lasted only one year, but it was a bitter experience for the indomitable is-

Painting of the brig "Agios Panteleimon," property of Ioannis G. Loukas of Salamina (Salamis Folklore Museum).

landers.

During the past 20 years or so, the islands have developed into popular vacation spots not only for Athenian holidaymakers but for people from other parts of Greece as well. They also attract their share of foreign tourists.

Painting of the brig "Poseidon" (below) and its figure-head (above), property of Pavlos Hatzianargiros of Spetses; this ship was built in 1814 (Spetses Museum).

Salamina

Name

The island's name (*Salamis*), as mentioned by Homer, is said to be derived from the Phoenician *salam*, meaning peace or tranquillity. Modern scholars, however cite the names *Pityoussa* (from the abundance of pine-trees: pitys in ancient Greek means pine-tree), *Cychreia* (from the mythical King Cychreas), *Sciras* (= rocky appearance, or Scirus, a mythical hero of Megara), *Kolouris* (from Cape Koulouris, where the ancient city stood, as mentioned by the scholar and poet Callimachus, 310-240 BC), among others.

Mythology

Greek myth-makers bestowed many beautiful myths on the islands of the Argosaronic Gulf, about their names and local heroes. The Saronic Gulf received its name from the mythical king of Troezen, Saron, who was a famous hunter, but was drowned in the waters of the Gulf while hunting a deer.

Salamis got its name from the nymph Salamis, daughter of the Corinthian River Asopus. Poseidon fell in love with her, and their son was the first mythical king of Salamis, Cychreas, who was half man and half fish! His daughter, Glauce, married Telamon.

Telamon and Peleas, sons of Endeis and the legendary king of Aegina, Aeacus, were jealous of their half-brother Phocus. The traveller Pausanias (2nd century AD) tells us that while Telamon was practising discus-throwing, his mother urged him to hit Phocus with the discus, and he was killed. Their father Aeacus banished Telamon and Peleas from the island. The story goes that Telamon returned one night secretly, dug a grave for Phocus and asked his father to forgive him. Aeacus would not let him set foot on land, so Telamon piled a mound of earth in the harbour and stated his case from there. His confession was not satisfactory, and, although as a father Aeacus would have like to have forgiven the murderer, he could not bring himself to do so.

Telamon eventually came back to live permanently on Salamis. He married Glauce and became king of the island. By his second marriage with Eriboea, Telamon had Ajax, who led the Salaminians and Megarians in the Trojan War (Homer, *Iliad*, III, 228). Another story goes that Heracles, who was a friend of Telamon, took the infant Ajax in his arms, covered him with his lion-skin and begged Zeus to make him immortal. But he left his armpit uncovered. As poet Sophocles tells it in his tragedy *"Ajax the Whip-Bearer"* (450-422 BC), after Ajax lost the contest for Achilles' arms, he went mad and whipped the rams, believing them to be the Atreidae and Odysseus (who had won the arms). When he came to his senses, he was not able to bear the shame and committed suicide by falling on his sword. Ajax was worshipped in Salamis; the Aeanteia, in which the Athenians also took part, were celebrated in his honour.

The Greeks had the statues of the Aeacidae in their ships during the historic Battle of Salamis, because they believed they would bring them victory. The historian Herodotus tells that during the battle the Athenians saw the shades of armed men coming from Aegina with their arms held high to protect the Greek triremes. Cychreas fought the Persians in the form of a snake. There was also a goddess who encouraged the men during the battle.

History

The island was inhabited as far back as Neolithic times, as shown by the artefacts found all along its southern coast.

Due to its privileged geographic position, it was often a bone of contention between the great city-states of the time,

Grave stele from 340 BC which portrays a hoplite with his hand on the head of a child. Behind them stands the hoplite's father (National Archaeological Museum).

who wanted to occupy it. It prospered in Mycenean times, when it was under the supervision of the Dryopians of Aegina.

During the Archaic period, Salamis grew into one of Greece's powerful economic and commercial centres, under the supervision of the Athenians. In historical times, possession of the island became a cause for discord between the Athenians and the Megarians; it was resolved in 604 BC, on the instigation of the Athenian legislator Solon, when the Athenians reoccupied the island. They established cleruchs there, administered by a powerful governor.

When at the beginning of the 5th century BC the Persian fleet sailed into the Aegean, the Salaminians offered no resistance and willingly cooperated with the Persians, to preserve their commercial dealings with the ports of Asia Minor. Ten years after their defeat at Marathon, the Persians attempted to attack Greece for a second time. As Herodotus tells us, it was the first time in history that such a powerful, well-organised military force was assembled. About 380 Greek warships, manned by 85,000 troops, were arrayed against the Persians' 1,200 warships and 2,500 auxiliary vessels manned by 300,000 troops. The Persians also had 700,000 footsoldiers and cavalry.

Leader of the campaign was Xerxes himself; his general was Mardonius. They set out in the spring of 480 BC from Sardis, capital of Lydia in Asia Minor, and after crossing the Hellespont, began their march down through Greece, occupying the city-states they met on their way with little or no resistance. In September of the same year the Persian army defeated the Spartan King Leonidas and his 300 men at Thermopylae and continued unimpeded on to Athens. The Delphic oracle advised that Greece would be saved by wooden walls. So the Greeks, united under the Athenian Themistocles and the Spartan Thrasybulus, with the Spartan Euribiades as commander of the fleet, assembled their forces at Salamis. With them were the Salaminians (12 ships), the Aeginetans, Corinthians, Megarians, Plataeans and Thebans (Spetsiots and Hydraeans may also have taken part). The commanders disagreed on whether the battle should take place at Salamis or the isthmus of Corinth. Themistocles, who knew how heavy and sluggish the Persian ships were, sent his slave Sicinnus to Xerxes to advise him to cut off the Greek fleet before it could sail towards the isthmus.

That is what happened, and Xerxes, sure of his victory, set his silver throne at the base of Mt. Aegaleo (Keratsini) and watched the battle from there. On September 22 of 480 BC, the biggest clash of the fleets took place in the strait between ancient Kolouris (near Cape Pounta in

Ambelakia Bay), near Cape Cynosura (Psitalia islet), Cape Ceramus (Drapetsona), Keratsini and Amphiale (Perama), where the Greeks routed the Persians. That evening, the wreckage of Persian ships and corpses floated in the waters of the Saronic Gulf.

The Battle of Salamis was decisive, not only because it delivered Greece from the Persian menace, but also because it saved the whole of Europe from Asian barbarism. After the battle, the victors dedicated a Phoenician trireme at the temple of Poseidon in Sunium. The names of the victorious cities were inscribed on a gold tripod which was dedicated at Delphi.

The day the historic Battle of Salamis was fought, the tragic poet Euripides was born on the island, according to various inscriptions found there. Greece's other two great tragic poets were also present at the battle: Aeschylus fought in it, and Sophocles, an adolescent at the time, led the chorus of boys who sang the paean after the battle.

During the Peloponnesian War, the Salaminians, naturally allies of Athens, were attacked in 429-428 BC by the Spartan general Brasidas. After the peace negotiated by Antalcidas in 387 BC between the Spartans and the Persians, Salamis once again passed into Athenian hands and cleruchs were sent to settle there.

Salamis knew another period of prosperity, in which bronze coins were minted, during the 4th century BC. In 318 BC she defected from the Athenians and allied herself with the Macedonian King Cassandrus. When the Athenians again became masters of the island in 307 BC, they drove out the inhabitants, settled cleruchs on the island, took the defectors captive and sentenced the general in charge, Aeschetades, to death. The captives were freed by Cassandrus, but when he died, Salamis came under the leadership of the Achaean Confederation.

It was later sacked by the Macedonians and invaded by pirates.

In Roman times the island was essentially a dependency of Athens although it was officially governed by the Roman conquerors. During early Byzantine times, the capital was moved to Aeanteion. But the monk "Nikon the Repentant", writing in AD 998, refers to the town as abandoned (this is at variance with the existence of 10th-century churches and 11th-century sculpture). Later the island passed to the Venetians, and after the 12th century it became a base of operations for pirates.

During the difficult centuries of the Turkish occupation Salamis enjoyed special privileges, as its shipyards were famous for repairing and maintaining the bottoms of the Sultan's ships. At that time, trade and shipping also flourished.

Salamis took part in the Orloff uprising, under Mitromaras (M. Lekkas), and flew the Russian flag. During the 1821 War of Independence, the Salaminians joined the Friendly Society of Greek patriots, and many of them were members of the Revolutionary hero Georgios Karai-

A Koulouriote sailor; charcoal drawing by I. Trikalitis, 1922 (Salamina Folklore Museum).

Concert in the Euripidio Theatre

skakis' hand-picked corps.

In modern times, Salaminians earn their living in the Perama-Piraeus industrial zone, in the dockyards and in shipping and fishing (Greece's largest fishermen's cooperative is in Salamina). The island has also boasted important men of the arts and letters, from ancient times (the tragic poet Euripides) up to the present (Professor P. Fourikis, the artist P. Lembessis, the poet from Lefkada A. Sikelianos, who spent his summers and wrote many of his works on Salamina, the play-wright D. Bogris, the great bard and writer of folk songs and their lyrics G. Papasideris, the professor and archaeologist D. Pallas and the folklorist N. Saltaris).

Tour of the Island

Salamina has an area of 95 square kilometres and a population of 23,000; it lies just one nautical mile from Piraeus. Its proximity to Attica has given it a dense population, but has altered its island character; it is an extension of Piraeus both physically and administratively.

In **Paloukia**, next to a playground, an outdoor nautical museum containing torpedoes and cannon has been set up. In 1878 the naval dockyard was moved from Poros to Faneromeni on Salamina, and in 1881 to Paloukia. To the right of the harbour lies the islet of Agios Georgios (it has been identified with the larger of the two Pharmacuses islands, reputed site of Circe's grave). The Church of Agios Georgios was built on the foundations of an early byzantine basilica dating from

Foundations of buildings are all that remain of the ancient city of Salamis.

the 6th century.

Near Cape Pounta, between **Kamatero** and **Ambelakia**, lie the ruins of the town of Kolouris dating from historical times. Part of the 4th-century BC wall and foundations of buildings have been preserved. There are also ruins of buildings on the sea-bottom in the bay, where the ancient port stood. On the hillside rising behind the newly-built Church of the Panagia, a small rectangular structure was found, believed to have been a Macedonian tomb for a mass burial after a battle or epidemic. The town was probably abandoned sometime between the first century BC and the first century AD, after the fall of Athens.

The road continues on to **Selinia**, with hotels, restaurants and tavernas. A turnoff to the left just before Selinia leads down to the shipyards, where the tomb of the Greeks killed in the Battle of Salamis was constructed.

The island's capital, **Salamina** or **Koulouri**, as it is commonly known, is a modern town, bustling with life, particularly during the summer months. On Patris

Even though present-day Salamina has lost its local style of architecture, several neo-classical homes still adorn its capital, Koulouri.

hill the "Euripidio" was built in 1993; it is an open-air theatre where a Panhellenic

The Church of Agios Nikolaos can be seen in this view of Koulouri.

The splendid neo-classical building of the Euripi-des Association.

Poetry Competition is held in memory of

Local costumes (the second a bride's) and a loom (Folklore Museum)

the Greek poet A. Sikelianos. From here you can enjoy the view out over the bay at sunset. Of the island's 10 mills, the two on Mili hill have been restored. Chamber tombs have been discovered in the area, which confirm that it was inhabited from prehistoric times.

Built into one of the inside walls of the Church of Agios Dimitrios is a plaque commemorating the temporary burial in its courtyard of the hero Karaiskakis on April 23, 1827, after he was killed in the Battle of Phaleron. There is an important fresco in the Church of Agios Minas.

On Akti Karaiskaki the building is still standing where Karaiskakis had his head-quarters. In the neo-classical building be-longing to the Community Cultural Centre "Euripides" (1958) are housed the Folk-lore Museum and a library containing 3,500 volumes. Here you will see rare lo-cal costumes, household utensils, farming implements, paintings of ships, etc. Opening hours are 5:00-8:00 pm daily in winter and 6:00-9:00 pm in summer. The Archaeological Museum, with 4th century BC grave stelae, is temporarily housed in a building next to the Church of Agios Nikolaos (opening hours 9:00 am-2:30 pm daily). The museum will soon move to the Kapodistriako Elementary School.

The restored 18th-century windmill on Mili hill

In Faneromeni Avenue, a few meters from Boskos Square, stands the Church of Panagia tou Boskou or Katharou housing frescos from 1758. Near the intersection with the road leading to the Ble Limanaki (= Blue Port) stands the Byzantine Church of Agios Grigorios dating from the 10th century, to which a narthex was added in the 13th century.

The island's largest and most important Byzantine monastery is the nunnery of Faneromeni. Tradition has it that sometime in the mid-1700s the Megarian peasant L. Kanellos dreamed that the Virgin ordered him to renovate the ruined Church of the Metamorphosis of the Saviour (ca. 15th century) on Salamina. It is also said that the poor peasant crossed the sea from Megalo Pefko to Salamina using his overcoat as a raft. There he found the miraculous icon of Panagia Faneromeni. The Church's heavy wooden double door still has holes made by Turkish bullets when the Turkish Marshal Kioutahis tried to take the nunnery. The interior of its 13th-century church, a three- aisled domed basilica, is completely covered in 3,597 superb, albeit time-worn, frescos painted in 1735 by the Argive hagiographer of the Cretan-Athos School, G. Markos and his pupils. Particularly imposing is the representation of the Second Coming. Next to the nunnery's main church, the Church of Agios Nikolaos has been added; it contains icons as well as the skull of St. Laurentius. South of the nunnery grounds stands the Chapel of Agii Apostoli which has been converted into a small ecclesiastical museum. The nunnery offers a hostel and workshops

View of the Faneromeni Monastery and the façade of its church

The Byzantine Church of Agios Ioannis Kalivitis

The house where the poet Sikelianos stayed

where some of the nuns paint icons, make candles and weave textiles. It holds a grand festival on 23-25 August. Near the sea is the house where the poet A. Sikelianos stayed.

In pine-clad **Moulki (Aeanteion)**, site of an extensive Early Helladic settlement,

The Monastery of Agios Nikolaos Lemonion

one can see the Churches of the Metamorphosis of the Saviour and the Kimissi tis Theotokou (= Assumption of the Virgin), dating from the 11th or 12th century.

On Cape Petritis is Kavo-Petritis or Fokas cave, to which Euripides' biographers claim the poet retreated to write his 92 dramas, of which only 19 have come down to us.

Five kilometres beyond Moulki, on Mt. Stavros in the southwestern part of the island, stands the monastery of Agios Nikolaos Lemonion. The area is lush with vegetation; the spring and the ancient torrent Bocarus once watered the lemon-trees for which the area is named. The exact date the monastery was founded is unknown, but it was renovated in 1742. The monastery's church is a single-aisled

The Telamon Sailing Club

basilica. Its walls are ornamented with 6 decorative plates from Rhodes. Two Byzantine marble slabs from Moulki bearing bas-reliefs, dating from the 10th-11th centuries, have been built into the church's facade. The monastery has had cells and a hostel since 1966. Just opposite is the 10th-century Byzantine Church of Agios Ioannis Kalivitis.

The locale west of the **Peristeria** beacon is called *Kolones* (= columns), from the ruins of the island's very ancient town which appears to have been inhabited up to the end of the 7th century BC. According to Strabo, this town was called *Salamis* and the island *Cychreia*. Recently the cave near the ruined town was systematically explored by the archaeologist G. Lolos and the Department of Palaeoanthopology and Speleology. The finds (vessels, stone tools, Mycenean lamps, jewellery, Greco-Roman and Frankish coins, etc.) have revealed that it was first inhabited in the Late Neolithic Era and remained in use down through 7 ages.

Pausanias visited ancient Cychreia - some believe that he was referring to the town from historical times on the Bay of Ambelakia – and saw the marketplace, temples dedicated to Ajax, Aesculapius, Dionysus and Artemis, a stoa, an exedra, a gymnasium and a theatre. As far as the ruins of an aqueduct are concerned, it is said that Cychreus' successor, Ajax, kept a mistress from Corinth in his palace; he brought water from the Stymphalian lake for her to drink and bathe in. It is also said

The ruins of an ancient tower in the town of Cychreia

that there is a cave that runs under the sea as far as Corinth, connecting Salamis with the Stymphalian lake.

Salamina is ideal for lively night life of all types. Excursions are organised to Aegina and Angistri. Celebrated in the traditional way are the New Year, Carnival and the *"Fisherman's Festival"* (on the Saturday in August when the moon is full). The municipal philharmonic, the Salamina Girls' Lyceum and the Tina Begni and Paloukia dance companies participate in all the town's cultural events and provide us with a picture of the island's rich folkloric tradition. Turtle-doves and quail are hunted in Kanakia. The Salamina Nautical Club offers a school of oarsmanship. Best for swimming and fishing is the island's south coast, in particular the pebble beaches at Kanakia, Peristeria, Iliakti, Perani and Giala. On the north coast, one can swim at the beaches of Psili Ammos and Faneromeni.

Aegina

Mythology

The ancient traveller Pausanias gives us some information on Aegina and her famous heroes. The nymph Aegina was the daughter of the River Asopus and sister of Salamis. She fell victim to the erotic passion of Zeus, who is said to have transformed himself either into an eagle or into fire in order to abduct her. He took her to the uninhabited island of Oinone or Oinopia and had Aeacus by her.

Her inconsolable father, in his search for his daughter, came to Corinth, which was suffering from a severe drought. He made water flow from a dry spring, whereupon the King of Corinth Sisyphus disclosed the name of his daughter's abductor. It is said that when Asopus finally found her, Zeus forced him to return to his river-bed. To punish Sisyphus for letting the cat out of the bag, Zeus condemned him after his death to push a boulder up a hill, never reaching the top. Another version says that he transformed Aegina into an island and himself into a rock.

So that his child would not be alone, the father of the gods turned the island's ants into people, and that is why the Aeginetans were called *Myrmidons* (myrmix = ant). The Myrmidons were legendary Achilles' famous warriors in the Trojan War.

Aeacus married Endeis, daughter either of the Centaur Chiron or of the brigand Sciron, and had two sons by her, Peleus and Telamon. Later Aeacus fell in love with the daughter of Nereus, Psamathe, who transformed herself into a seal in order to evade him. But Aeacus was not deterred in the least by her metamorphosis and had a son, Phocus, by her. When Phocus grew up, he won all the athletic games and his brothers were jealous of him. Pausanias says that they was egged on by Endeis, who didn't like him and had never forgiven her husband for cheating on her. So one day while Phocus was practising discus-throwing, Telamon hit him in the head with a discus and killed him. The brothers hid his body in the woods, where Aeacus found it a few days later. Furious, he drove the two young men off the island.

Telamon became King of Salamis. The story goes that he returned to Aegina clandestinely one night, built a tomb for Phocus and asked his father to forgive him. His confession did not satisfy Aeacus; against his fatherly instincts, he would not forgive the murderer.

Peleus took refuge in Thessaly. After many adventures he married the nymph Thetis and had Achilles by her.

From the grammarian Apollodorus of Athens (2nd century BC) we learn that as a result of that act and many others Aeacus became a respected figure in antiquity and was worshipped on the island as a hero. Ancient authors refer to him as one of the three judges of Hades, together with Radamanthys and Minos. The Roman sage Pliny the Elder (23 BC-AD 79) accredits him with the discovery of silver. Aeacus, however, also enjoyed the esteem of the gods. According to the lyric poet Pindar (4th century BC), he collaborated with Apollo and Poseidon in building the walls of Troy. When they were finished, three snakes tried to crawl over the walls, but two of them died immediately. The third scaled the wall, and Apollo

The Church of Taxiarhes, built near the sanctuary of Hellanian Zeus on Mt. Oros.

prophesied that this meant that a descendant of Aeacus would conquer Troy.

Another story goes that once when the whole Peloponnese was afflicted by a drought and crowds of pilgrims were pouring into Aegina to pray to Zeus to send rain, the priestess at Delphi pronounced that the gods would only heed the pleas of Aeacus. So he climbed to Aegina's highest mountaintop, Oros, and beseeched Zeus to make it rain. His prayer was heard, and Aeacus built a temple there in honour of the god.

His descendants, the Aeacidae, were famous heroes of the Argonauts' expedition and the Trojan War. Their statues were kept in Aegina and were held to be sacred. Because they were believed to ensure victory, the Greeks took them with them to the historic Battle of Salamis. Herodotus tells us that during the Battle, the Athenians saw the shades of armed men flying from Aegina with arms raised to protect the Greek triremes.

Aphaea (Apha) was a Creto-Mycenean fertility goddess. Pausanias relates that Zeus and Carme had a daughter Britomartis whom the goddess Artemis fav-

Watercolour of the facade of the tomb of the Leucadians in Pella (drawn by A. Kountouras and painted by H. Lefakis); *it depicts the three judges of Hades together with Hermes: from left, Minos, Hermes, Aeacus (seated) and Radamanthys.*

oured because she loved hunting. The girl's beauty, however, often got her into trouble, as it caused Minos, King of Crete, to fall in love with her. In her attempt to evade him, she fell into the sea and got tangled up in the nets of some fishermen, one of whom fell in love with her! So she jumped into the sea again and came ashore on Aegina. The sailors, who had followed her, saw her disappear into the island's grove (where the temple stands) as though by divine intervention, and they named her Aphaea (= the one who vanished). Aphaea hid in a cave in the northeastern corner of the temple grounds. She became a local deity identified with Athena.

History

The island was first settled in the Neolithic Era (3500-2600 BC). This is proved by the stone tools and many clay pots found in the towns founded by settlers from the Peloponnese on Kolona hill and in Messagros. Early Helladic settlements (2500-2000 BC) have also been identified; they were used as way-stations between the Peloponnese and the Cyclades.

Around 2100 BC, at the time when the powerful Early Helladic centre at Lerna was in decline, a new population factor made its appearance, arriving from the north. These Middle Helladic people settled in Aegina, which became a powerful bulwark defending Attica from raiders from the sea, but failed to develop into a naval power because of Minoan Crete's supremacy on the seas.

The mountain-dwelling Dryopians, the predominant element in the population in the Late Helladic Era, founded a new settlement at Oros in Aegina; they are said to have introduced the worship of Hellanian Zeus (sender of rain) to southern Greece.

Late in the 13th century BC Aegina took part in the 10-year Trojan War, send-

A broad-hipped Neolithic marble female figurine from Aegina (National Archaeological Museum)

ing more ships than any of the other islands of the Argosaronic Gulf. Around the end of the Mycenean Era (approximately 1170 BC), Aegina, now great and powerful, was attacked by the Myceneans, who subjugated the inhabitants, leaving the island sparsely populated for the next three centuries, up to the time of the Dorian invasion (1100 BC).

In the mid-7th century BC, the Calaurian Amphictyony – whose centre was the temple of Calaurian Poseidon – came onto the scene; Aegina became a member. At that time the island had close commercial ties to Epidaurus, to which it was subjugated after 950 BC. When the progressive tyrant of Argos, Pheidon, joined the Calaurian Amphictyony, he found a way to establish maritime trade stations in Aegina, which dominated trade on the seas. Around 650 BC, he minted the *"Chelone"*, the first silver coin in the Greek world, and established standard weights. Aegina developed into a powerful economic and commercial centre of Greece and became renowned for its fine pottery. This economic prosperity led to

The "Chelone" (Numismatic Museum)

the construction of many sanctuaries and public buildings.

Herodotus mentions that the fugitive Samian oligarchs living in Hydra in 528/526 BC attempted piratical raids on mighty Aegina. The Aeginetans made a counter-attack and thus the Samians departed for Cydonia (present-day Hania) in Crete. Cydonia was later destroyed by the Aeginetans themselves, to secure a route to Egypt. For the next century Aegina remained autonomous and powerful.

When at the beginning of the 5th century BC the Persian fleet sailed into the Aegean, Aegina offered no resistance and voluntarily cooperated with the Persians, to prevent her commerce with the ports of Asia Minor from being cut off. Aegina's rise was arrested when the Athenian fleet came to dominate the seas after the Persian Wars. When Xerxes began his second campaign against the Greeks, the Aeginetans concentrated their naval forces at Salamis.

The Athenians learned that the Aeginetans wanted to ally themselves with the Corinthians against them (due to the expansion of Athenian trade to the ports of Italy), and the two fleets clashed at Cecryphaleia (present-day Angistri) in 459 BC. The victorious Athenians obliged the Aeginetans to tear down their city walls and pay exorbitant taxes each year.

(Pericles characteristically called Aegina the *"eye-gum of Piraeus"*).

In the Peloponnesian War, the Aeginetans, being both Dorians and oligarchs, naturally sided with Sparta. During the very first year of the war (431 BC) they were attacked by 100 Athenian triremes. The capital was occupied, depopulated and resettled by Athenian cleruchs, among them the comic poet Aristophanes (452-385 BC) and Ariston, father of Plato. The Aeginetans were led by their Spartan allies to Thyrea (present-day Astros Kinourias) and remained there until the end of the war in 404 BC. In one of its raids, the Athenian fleet occupied Thyrea and, according to Thucydides, many Aeginetan refugees were transported to Attica and put to death. When the disastrous civil war came to an end in 404 BC, the Spartan Lysander gathered the remaining Aeginetans together and sent them home. During the Corinthian War (395-386 BC), Aegina became a base of the Spartans.

Under the Macedonians, some of the island's public buildings were repaired. After the death of Alexander the Great, Aegina joined the Achaean and later the Aetolian League. In 210 BC it was sold for 30 talents to the King of Pergamon, Attalus I. Some buildings were erected then and the town's sanctuaries were repaired. Because of its mild winters, many Pergamene kings and eminent Romans took up residence on the island. When Pausanias visited Aegina, which had dwindled to insignificance under the Roman occupation (133 BC-AD 395), many works of art had already been stolen by the Pergamenes.

It is also said that when Nero decided to dig a canal across the isthmus of Corinth in AD 64, the Aeginetans panicked because of an old Egyptian prophecy which said that if the isthmus were severed the waters of the Gulf of Corinth would flood the whole Saronic Gulf. So the digging of the canal was postponed!

The hill where Aegina's medieval capital, Palea Hora, was built

In Byzantine times the island belonged to the Theme of Greece, and was a bishop's see. During the 3rd century trade began to revive and its population was increased by an influx of inhabitants of the surrounding areas which were coming under attack by Goths and Herulians.

During the 6th century, Arab pirates appeared in the Argosaronic Gulf and refugees once again gathered on Aegina. By the 9th century Saracen pirates from Crete were swarming over the coasts of the Aegean, capturing and selling the inhabitants into slavery, and those Aeginetans who remained on the island moved inland and founded the town of Palea Hora or Aegena. The coast was abandoned for a century and the harbours filled with earth.

After the break-up of the Byzantine empire, Aegina was to go to the Venetians but instead it was handed over to Galea Malatesta and then, together with the town of Karistos (Evia), to the Frankish Baron Ravano della Carceri. After 1317 it passed to the Catalans through intermarriage and they kept it until 1451.

The following year their family voluntarily became subjects of Venice out of fear of the Turks who had repeatedly attacked the island.

The worst catastrophe, when 6000 islanders were taken prisoner, was brought about in October 1537 by the terrible pirate Barbarossa. The island was deserted and its southeastern coast resettled by Arvanite farmers and Greek settlers from the Peloponnese. In 1540 the Turks and Venetians signed a peace pact and *Ekine* (Aegina) was handed over to the Turks. The remaining inhabitants once again congregated in Palea Hora.

In September of 1654 Morosini occupied and sacked the island. When the war between the Turks and Venetians in Crete was over, Aegina passed first to the Turks and then in 1687 back to the Venetians. It remained a Venetian possession until 1718, when it was finally ceded to the Turks in the Pasarovich treaty of July 21.

After 1800, Palea Hora was abandoned and the inhabitants returned to their original capital (present-day Aegina). In 1821, about 400 Aeginetans took part in the revolution against the Turks.

On November 11, 1826, Aegina became the seat of the administrative committee of A. Zaimis, and on January 12, 1828, of the government of Ioannis Kapodistrias, which was recognised by the Great Powers. Thus it became the temporary capital of the country, and in October of 1828 the *"Phoenix"*, the first coin of the newly-formed state, was minted there. Many important public and private buildings (Greek and French printing-offices, a lithographer's office, schools, an orphanage) were erected and the island became a political and cultural centre of that era. Numbers of refugees, mainly from Asia Minor, settled on Aegina.

Aegina Town

Aegina has an area of 85 square kilometres, a population of 11,270 and lies at a distance of 17 nautical miles from Piraeus. It is close enough to Athens to be one of its suburbs.

The present-day harbour was the ancient city's commercial harbour. (A sanctuary of Aphrodite Pontia (of the Deep Sea), Euplia (of Good Sailing) or Limenia (of the Harbour) – mentioned by Pausanias – is said to have stood here; she was the protectress of navigation and of sailors.) Small additions were made during Roman and Venetian times and while Kapodistrias' government was located here. Today it is a bustling, noisy meeting-place of quaint fishermen selling the day's catch and grocers with boats for shops, from whom you can buy fresh fruit and vegetables.

Next to the harbour was the ancient town's military harbour, which some experts have identified with the naval port built for additional protection in 482 BC; it was not easily discerned from the open sea and was therefore known as the hidden harbour. Others believe it was locat-

View of the waterfront in Aegina. The impression the town makes on the visitor is that of a small Greek 19th-century town.

The Pistachio-tree (Pistacia vera) is a member of the Anacardiaceae family. The pistachio was originally round like a hazel-nut, but gradually took on its pen-nib shape.

The Aeginetan clay pots were in such demand in ancient markets that they provoked the envy of the Athenians, who referred to them contemptuously as "Aeginaean goods" (metaphorically, anything of little value).

ed near the Kolona public beach. Still in existence are portions of the moles and the sheds where ships were kept; it has been estimated that they sheltered around 60 triremes.

No one must leave Aegina without buying some of the locally-grown pistachios, cultivated with care by people to whom mass production is anathema, who possess secrets unknown to modern technology. The first pistachio trees were brought here from Syria by a merchant named N. Peroglou a century ago, and they flourished due to the composition of the island's soil and its dry climate.

The main road by the waterfront is off-

Narrow, shady streets with old neo-classical mansions overhung with geraniums and other greenery, and little coffee shops, ouzo bars, tavernas serving fresh fish and night clubs make up the picture of the town.

The chapel of Agios Nikolaos Thalassinos at the harbour entrance

limits to vehicles on summer nights. For getting around town, choose a flower-be-decked one-horse carriage from those parked next to the jetty. The souvenir shops are busy at all hours of the day. Outstanding among the island's original gift items are the traditional Aeginetan water-jugs, which were used to carry and keep water cool: in former times the island had a water problem. Of the 48 potters who once worked there, today only four continue to ply the craft of their ancient forefathers.

Worth visiting on the waterfront is the chapel of Agios Nikolaos Thalassinos (first mentioned in 1693).

The town fans up from the harbour; some of its old neo-classical mansions have been restored and are rented out in single rooms to visitors. Of architectural importance are the Vogiatzis and A. Likouris (formerly K. Kanaris) homes.

In Sp. Rodi street stands the island's Museum of History and Folklore, which holds interesting exhibitions on the island's traditional life, as well as art exhibitions, lectures and seminars.

Close by the Church of Agios Nikolaos is one of the island's oldest medieval buildings, the Tower of Marcellus, which became the seat of Greece's first post-Revolutionary government in 1826-29. Nowadays it is used as an exhibition hall, where the municipality sponsors exhibitions by well-known artists. Behind the tower is the old Liberopoulos home (now the property of P. Papaleonardos) and a little further on the Varvakis home, which now belongs to G. Protonotarios.

When Aegina became the first capital of modern Greece, it also became the centre of social life, and splendid public buildings and institutions sprang up. Still standing are Kapodistrias' Government House, also known as the *"Palace of Barbagiannis"*. It is a modest two-story building erected soon after Kapodistrias arrived in town. The second floor housed the residence and office of the governor, and it was used for various purposes after the government was transferred to Nauplio. In the courtyard of Government House stands a building erected during the German occupation which now houses the Historical Archives of Aegina and the Kapodistrian Public Library whose collection numbers 30,000 volumes.

When Palea Hora was destroyed and the capital moved back to the harbour town, one of the island's loveliest churches was erected; it is the Metropolis (Kimissi tis Theotokou), built in 1806. It was here that the governor was welcomed amidst festivities in 1828.

In 1830 Kapodistrias built the Eynardian College of Education in the courtyard of the Metropolis with funds donated by his close friend the French philhellene Jean Eynard. (The two had met as young men in Geneva, when Kapodistrias was laying the framework of the Swiss state!) The rectangular Doric building had a portico decorated with pediments; it was the first neo-classical building of Greece. It was soon scheduled to house the Public Library. A later addition to the same area was the Preparatory School.

Another building dating from Kapodistrias' era (1828) is the rectangular Orphanage behind the Saronikos playing-field. It was a huge edifice for its time (10,000 square meters)! Five hundred orphans lived here and learned reading, writing and practical crafts and trades. It was also the first building to house a national library, archaeological museum, school of music, agricultural and military schools and a national printing office. Later it was converted into a prison. In future it will house the Museum of Aegina through the Ages.

It is not known where the newly-formed state's mint was housed. Its director, Alexandros Kontostavlos, bought the machinery from the mint of the Order of the Knights of Malta at a low price. In spite of doubts about the condition of this machinery, the first thin, brass coins were presented on July 18, 1829, at the Fourth National Assembly in Argos in an atmosphere of patriotic pride.

The road leading towards Agios Nektarios passes the rather unconventional Church of Faneromeni. For years it has stood here unfinished, meanwhile housing two underground churches in its basement, one dedicated to Agia Athanassia and the other to the Virgin.

On the other side of town, on **Kolona** hill, lies Aegina's prehistoric town. First to excavate the area were the English architect Charles Robert Cockerell in 1811, the Estonian traveller O. M. von Stackelberg and the German archaeologist A. Furtwängler in 1903. More recent excavations were begun in 1924 by the German archaeologist Gabriel Welter (1890-1954) and completed in 1966 by the German professor Hans Walter, director of the Bavarian Academy. They brought to light a unique phenomenon: eleven successive towns on the same site, clearly showing the development of systems of fortification in prehistoric times.

The first inhabitants of the area settled here around 3000 BC and the site – 250 m in length and 80 m in width – was not abandoned for 2000 years, in spite of being attacked many times. The 8 oldest towns were enclosed by walls and the remaining three had a wall in common with the town below. Most of the houses were built of sun-dried bricks on stone founda-

Experienced coachmen will show you the town's sights. Here, the Vogiatzis home, which has been termed a work of art.

tions; others were huts made of woven grass, rushes and clay, as were the flat roofs. Each new town was more advanced than the preceding one. For example, the third town contained a large two-story house, the fourth had an bronze foundry unique of its kind, and the fifth had roads and houses which were divided into rooms.

The final town stood at the edge of the

The pink tower of Marcellus (1802), possibly a revamped medieval fortress. To the left the Church of Agios Nikolaos can be seen.

island's present-day capital and was fortified with walls. When Pausanias visited
the island in 150 BC, many works of art
had already been stolen by the Pergamenes. According to the ancient traveller, the most renowned building of the
ancient city was the Doric temple of Apollo, built of porous stone in 520 BC. It was
erected on the site of the old settlement.
It was peripteral, with 6 columns on the
front and back and 11 on each side. Out
of a total of 30 columns only two are still
in existence in the opisthodomus, one of
which gave the area its name. The upper
part of the first (still standing today) fell
along with the architrave after 1765. In
1802 the second was laid flat in a storm.

During the 4th century AD, all the temples, among them Apollo's, were pulled
down as symbols of idolatry. In its place a
large building with a water tank was erected. Jews settled in the Karantina area,
and built a synagogue with a mosaic floor.

West of the temple the foundations of
the two smaller temples of Dionysus and
of Artemis can be seen, together with a
propylon, believed to belong to the Aea-
caeum dating from the Pergamene era
(210-133 BC). The Attaleion was also
built during that time. Archaeologists have
identified as the tomb of Phocus a circular
base dating from the late 6th century BC.
Further to the east was the Buleuterium,
a grandiose classical theatre – compara-
ble to the one at Epidaurus, according to
Pausanias – and behind it a stadium,
whose rows of stone seats were used in
the 3rd century AD to fortify the town.

*There was also a temple dedicated to
Delphinian Apollo, protector of seafarers.
In his honour games were held during the
month of Delphinium; their theme was
water. The contest was called hydrophori-
um or amphorites. In it young men filled
clay jugs with water from the Asopis foun-
tain (at present-day Kolona) and raced to*

*The column from the opisthodomus of the Doric temple of Apollo, built of porous stone in 520 BC; Pausanias
erroneously believed that it was a temple of Aphrodite of Good Sailing, but the main temples of Doric cities
were never dedicated to that goddess.*

the finish line carrying the jugs on their shoulders.

Other temples were dedicated to Heracles, Demeter, Athena, and one to Hecate, goddess of the moon. Great festivals were held in her honour, and her wooden statue was the work of the famous sculptor Myron. At the temple of Poseidon the festivals lasted 16 days. In his play *"Wasps"* the comic poet Aristophanes mentions the existence of an Aesculapium, where patients were left to be cured by the god himself!

Unfortunately, the Kolona Archaeological Museum has been closed for some time for repairs, depriving visitors of the chance to admire the island's finds, including pottery from all epochs, sculpture, pediments from the temples of Apollo and Aphaea, etc.

Rock tombs, most of them pillaged, have been found in the area around the town. The oldest date back to the 6th century BC. They consist of two or more asymmetric rooms where the dead were buried in stone or wooden sarcophagi covered with stone slabs. Other important tombs, also pillaged, date from the Pergamene era.

Kolona beach is a fine place to swim (its pine-shaded park is ideal for picnics), as are the small sandy inlets which indent the shore along the coastal road.

The coastal road to **Plakakia** passes the Wild Animal Treatment Centre, which cares for animals and birds, a sincere effort by young people deserving of support (Donations may be made to Account No. 241/745090-75 in the National Bank of Greece). Two kilometres from town is the house where the famous author Nikos Kazantzakis stayed as a guest in Aegina.

Worth visiting is the chapel of Agii Theodori, also known as *Omorfi Eklissia* (= beautiful Church), on the outskirts of town. Built in 1289, it is a single-aisled basilica constructed of huge slabs of porous stone from an ancient temple. At the office of the Archaeological Museum,

The public beach at Kolona

you can make an appointment to be let in to see the chapel's unique frescos depicting 15 scenes from the life of Christ.

A short distance to the south, in the **Asomati** area, stands the *"Red Castle"*, as the home of the English historian G. Finlay is known; it was here that Greece's first ever masked ball was held during the 1826 Carnival season.

Aegina - Souvala - Palea Hora - Agios Nektarios Monastery

The road in front of the Metropolis leads to the populous community of **Kipseli**, four km away, with traditional two-story houses and a lovely town square. Worth seeing is the old Church of Agios Nikolaos in Moulo, built on the site of a ruined ancient tower using building materials taken from it. Also worth visiting are the Churches of Agia Marina and Agios Ioannis in Pefko. Visitors to the area may swim at Kavouropetra. You can continue on to the seaside area of **Leonti** at a distance of 5 km, site of the original monastery of Hrissoleontissa before it was moved inland out of fear of pirates.

The same road now runs on to the farming town of **Vathi** 7 km away, and after another 8 km winds up at the small harbour of **Souvala**, a tourist resort in the making with a fine beach. (Souvala means a large open tank for collecting water.) The area boasts a warm sulphurous healing spring, said to be suit-

Souvala; when Palea Hora was capital of the island and Souvala its port.

able for gynaecological, dermatological and rheumatic complaints.

A turnoff from the seaside road to Vagia brings us to **Agii** (10 km), a village smothered in pine-trees, famous for its water-jug potters and the Church of the Apostle Crispus, a disciple of the Apostle Paul. Crispus came to Aegina to preach Christianity, came upon the village of Agrii (= savages) and renamed it Agii (= saints). The church commemorates him on December 4.

The seaside road now continues to **Vagia** (16 km), a tourist resort with a lovely sand beach. East of the village on Cape Koursospilia is the cave of the same name, from which corsairs organised their raids; it was later used by "pilots", experienced sailors who guided foreign sailing ships into the harbours of the Aegean; from here they served the port of Piraeus. Further south, on Cape Tourlos,

Vagia and its beach, sometimes windy, always lovely.

there are still shelters and cannon bases from the Second World War.

From Vagia we take the road to the farming community of **Messagros** (8.5 km), at the foot of Mt. Afea; the village has a long tradition in water-jug making. Here too is the characteristic folk-style house of A. Rodakis built in 1880.

On the way back to town you will encounter the village of **Kondos** (5.5 km). Here are two of Aegina's important sights, the Monastery of Agios Nektarios and the island's medieval capital, Palea Hora.

The pure white **Monastery of Agios Nektarios** (Agia Triada) was built in 1904-10 by the Metropolitan of Pentapoli Nektarios. This latter-day saint of Orthodoxy lived and was buried here. You can see a room containing his personal effects; there is also a hostel which welcomes the faithful. At the base of the hill stands the majestic Church of Agios Nektarios, built on the pattern of Agia Sofia in Constantinople. Its silver bell is the biggest ever made in Greece; it weighs three tons, has a height of 1.75 m and a diameter of 1.71 m. and is composed of a group of 10 bells!

Anastassios Kefalas was born in 1840 in Silivria, Thrace. As a child he worked after school in a tobacco factory in Constantinople. When he finished his studies he went to work as a teacher in Lithi, Hios. In 1876 he became a monk and a year later was ordained a deacon. He completed his studies at the University of Athens and became the Metropolitan of Pentapoli in 1889. When he returned to Greece he was assigned to Evia as a priest and later appointed head of the Rizareios School. At an advanced age he retired to the Monastery of Agia Triada, where he remained until the end of his life in 1920. He was canonised in 1961. His memory is honoured on November 9, when his remains are carried in a great procession.

Palea Hora was built on a precipitous rock, when in AD 896 the harbour town suffered a terrible invasion by Saracen pirates and the frightened inhabitants retreated toward the interior of the island. The locals aptly called it the second Mistras; narrow winding streets and steep flights of stairs led to the town's 365 churches dating from every period of its existence. Its inhabitants worked as merchants and seafarers, out of the ports of Souvala and Perdika. The town was continuously inhabited until 1800.

When strife broke out between the Sublime Porte and the Venetians, the Turkish Admiral Kemal Reis stormed the castle and enslaved its 2000 inhabitants (1502). In October 1537 the fearsome pirate Khayr al-Din Barbarossa wreaked havoc on the island, slaughtering the men and carrying 6000 women and children off to the slave markets. The only thing he respected was the churches, which however did not escape the Venetians in 1654.

Today the town is full of ruined houses

Tradition has it that the lush Messagros area was once part of the seabed. Senior potter Spiros Sklavenas can confirm this, as he sometimes finds sea-shells in his clay!

Like the temple of Aphaea in antiquity, the Monastery of Agios Nektarios is today a place of pilgrimage for the pious.

14th-century Church of Agios Nikolaos Mavrikas, off to the right of the road to Messagros; Stavros at the foot of the hill, where festivities are held on September 14 and where on Easter Monday the *"Great Easter Dance"* lives on; Agios Georgios Katholikos dating from 1533; Episkopi, the metropolis of Palea Hora, with the cell of St. Dionysios, once bishop of Aegina; Taxiarhis, dating from 1293, with an abundance of frescos and figures of Saints and an inscription dated January 7, 1801 affirming the townspeople's decision to return to the harbour town. There are many other churches with important frescos. A footpath from Episkopi leads to Kastro, built by the Venetians in 1654. There ruins of walls, windmills and cisterns can be seen. (Because the climb up the hill is quite tiring, visitors would be well advised to wear hats and take some cool water with them. Early morning and evening are the best times to make the ascent.)

and churches; only 40 of the latter are in fair condition and only 20 retain their frescos. Outstanding among them are the

The well-preserved Church of Episkopi, a domed basilica. Inset: the church's interior.

From Kondos, a road leads to the Monastery of Hrissoleontissa, on a green hill in the centre of the island. The Monastery originally stood in the Leonti area, but after repeated pirate attacks the monk Makarios decided, in about 1600, to move it further inland. In 1601 a crenelated three-story tower was erected, and in 1808 the monastery church was built. It was destroyed in 1885 together with a large library and archives. Today's visitor will marvel at the huge carved wooden altar-screen. The church holds a great celebration on August 15.

Hrissoleontissa Monastery. Its name indicates its one-time wealth (hrissos = gold); it once owned three quarters of Aegina's land!

Aegina - Temple of Aphaea - Agia Marina

Just before Agia Marina on the top of a pine-clad hill lie the ruins of the Doric **temple of Athena Aphaea** (11.5 km).

The region's first settlements came into being in Late Neolithic times, as Welter's excavations showed; together with the one at Kolona, they are the oldest on the island. Excavations have revealed that they had some connection with the inhabitants of the eastern Peloponnese.

The sanctuary site seems to have been used as a place of worship as far back as 1300 BC. Excavations in 1901 brought to light clay figures of women and animals in the place where Aphaea is said to have hidden. During the 7th-5th centuries BC, when the island was at the peak of its prosperity, three successive temples were built on the spot.

The first sanctuary was nothing more than a natural monument, of which only one narrow foundation has survived. Important finds from this era include clay pots.

Of the second, there are only traces of an altar on the east side: In 510 BC a great fire destroyed the temple's roof so completely that the Aeginetans tore it down, along with the sanctuary's other buildings. Around that time the sanctuary's tallest monument was erected, an imposing column supporting a marble sphinx. (The demonic winged creature was the sanctuary's guardian angel.)

The sanctuary took on its final form around 500-480 BC. Extensive earthworks raised it to a single level and allowed it to be enlarged, thus making it a unique achievement of its time. It was enclosed in a circular brick stone-based wall. The peripteral temple was built of soft porous stone; it had 6 columns on the ends and 12 on the sides (today 20 are standing). Besides the temple, the sanctuary contained the Propylaea, chambers where offerings were made, an altar, a service building for the priests, and baths. No additions were made after that, perhaps due to the island's economic decline.

Battles were pictured on both pediments of the main temple. In the centre a figure of Athena predominated. Tradition has it that one pediment depicted the abduction of the nymph Aegina by Zeus and other various battle scenes, of which no precise interpretation could be made.

When part of the eastern pediment was destroyed during the Persian Wars – perhaps by lightning – the irreparable fragments were buried, as was the custom in those times. The larger pieces were set up in the temple grounds. (These sculptures came to light in Furtwängler's excavations and are now on display in the National Archaeological Museum in Athens).

New sculpture depicting the siege, defence and sack of Troy, took the place of the old; again Athena figured at the centre of each pediment. The eastern pediment had to do with the victorious campaign of Telamon and his friend Heracles against the army of the King of Troy Laomedon, and the western one involved the campaign of Ajax, Teucrus and Achilles against Priam.

Unfortunately, these sculptures are not where they rightfully belong, because Cockerell and the German architect Baron Haller von Hallerstein, who discovered them in 1811, spirited them away, with the consent of the Turks, to English-occupied Zakinthos and later to Malta. After being auctioned off in Zakinthos and finally sold for 70,000 florins to Ludwig I, *prince of Bavaria, they were restored in Rome and transported to Munich, where they now adorn the Glyptotheque!*

Cockerell believed that the temples were dedicated to Athena, who is depicted prominently on both pediments. His theory was overturned in 1901, when Furtwängler discovered an archaic inscription in the foundation of the temple, which states that when Cleoitus was priest the foundation was laid for the temple of the local goddess Aphaea.

In the middle of the main temple a statue of Athena, slightly larger than life-size, stood on a pedestal. Her battle dress and weapons were bronze, and the visible parts of her body were made of marble. But after the discovery of the inscription which revealed that the temple belonged to Aphaea, at the right side of the bottom of the nave a simple limestone

The choice of a location for the temple of Aphaea was an excellent one. Thick pines encircle the temple, which commands a panoramic view of the sea. It awakens a feeling of religious piety in today's visitor, as it once did in the ancient pilgrim. The last temple to be built had many points in common with the two previous ones; its simplicity is enchanting.

pedestal was discovered, which had supported an ivory statue of Aphaea, fashioned in the Archaic style!

West of the temple there is a small museum with rare painted copies of the pediments from the second in the series of temples of Aphaea; it remains closed due to lack of staff!

The road runs down to the holiday resort of **Agia Marina** (14.5 km). When you enter the main street, you will understand why this is always a bustling place! There are souvenir shops, jewellers, hotel complexes and bungalows, restaurants serving international cuisine, cafeterias open all day long and finally the sweeping expanse of a fine sand beach, equipped with chairs, umbrellas, pedal boats, canoes and water-skis to rent, a real sports-lover's paradise. Every day this little old fishing village welcomes luxury cruise liners and yachts.

Those of you who decide to leave Agia Marina the same day – and I doubt

Head of a helmeted warrior from the eastern pediment of the temple of Aphaea, from Furtwängler's excavations of 1901 (National Archaeological Museum)

many will – will be compensated by the

View of the tourist resort of Agia Marina

Chapel in the picturesque village of Anitseo

rest of the itinerary. First you will encounter the village of **Alones**, lying in a green valley, with lovely little tavernas (17.5 km). The seaside road continues on to the old village of **Kilindros** and winds up at the little port of **Portes**, which served the ancient town of Lazarides.

Aegina - Sanctuary of Hellanian Zeus

The verdant Oros area took its name

The Byzantine church in the Taxiarhes Monastery on Mt. Profitis Ilias

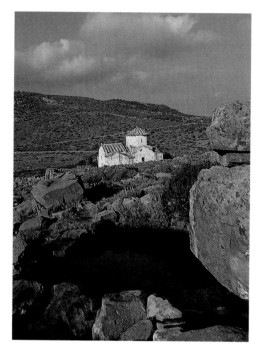

from Mt. Oros or Profitis Ilias, which is the island's highest point at 532 m. It is still touristically unexploited, but offers beautiful traditional villages such as **Kapotides**; **Lazarides**, where a Mycenean necropolis with a wealth of grave goods was uncovered; **Pahia Rahi**, with the superb 17th-century Church of Agios Dionysios; **Anitseo**; the little mountain village of **Kanakides**, with only a few remaining inhabitants; and **Vlahides**.

On the peak of **Mt. Oros**, commanding a view of the whole island, there was a sanctuary in historical times, where it is said that Aeacus established the worship of Hellanian Zeus. The climb up Mt. Oros is rather taxing. At its base, an inscription informs us of the existence of a small sanctuary dedicated to the Coliadae nymphs. A Pergamene-era set of stone steps, once lined with offerings, leads up to the sanctuary. We come out onto a level place, where the church of the Byzantine Monastery of Taxiarhes still stands. In 1829-30 the historian A. Moustoxidis discovered the wall which enclosed the sanctuary of the nymphs. Later, Welter found traces of a fortified farming settlement of the 13th century BC. The altar was built in the Geometrical era. A staircase 7 m wide led to a large building, possibly a hostel, of which all that have survived are the bases of three rows of columns which supported the roof. The foundations of a small stoa and two cisterns have also been preserved.

Aegina - Perdika

The road along the coast is lined with cafeterias and sandy beaches shaded by eucalyptus trees. It will lead you to the seaside settlement of **Faros**, with some of the island's loveliest neo-classical buildings, among them the stately home of A. Kontostavlos, that of S. Trikoupis (now the Floros home) and the old Voulgaris home, where Kapodistrias lived. Another such settlement is **Marathonas**.

It was in the small semi-circular Bay of Marathonas that the Greek ships gathered after the Battle of Salamis so that the victors could divide up the spoils. The same bay was used by the Venetian fleet and later by the European allies in the 1821 Revolution. And here the first cannon-fire was heard from Greek and allied ships as they welcomed Greece's first officially recognised government of Kapodistrias, along with the Greek flag!

Just before Perdika a turnoff to the left leads to **Sfendouri**. Most of the area's interest, however, is focused on **Perdika**; it is a fishing village which has been evolving during recent years into a holiday centre boasting several hotels. Nevertheless, it preserves an Aegean flavour unique on the island. The surrounding countryside, in contrast to the rest of the island, is a barren moonscape. It is illegal to hunt the partridges (= perdikes) which gave the area its name.

During the Turkish occupation the

The Faros area: in Aegina you will notice that most people prefer to use one of the island's myriad rented bicycles.

"kerkezi", skilful local sailors, smuggled in goods in small sailing-ships, which they hid in Fokospilia Cave on **Moni** islet. You can visit the islet in boats from Perdika. Drenched in greenery, it has been declared a biotope supporting a species of wild goat, *Capra aegagrus*, very similar to the wild goat of Crete (*rupricapra rupricapra*).

Luxury vessels are moored in Perdika's spacious marina so that their passengers can sample the freshly-caught fish and seafood in the tavernas lining the waterfront.

Angistri

A small, pine-covered island, very close to Aegina, Angistri has an area of 13 square kilometres, of which 9 are forested and 4 are farmed. It lies at a distance of 22 nautical miles from Piraeus. In ancient times it was known variously as *Pityoussa* and *Cecryphaleia*. We also know that in 323 BC a section of the island northeast of Skala sank into the sea following an earthquake.

The quaint tavernas, the great number of rooms to rent, the absence of automobiles, the night-life and the isolated rocky shores washed by crystalline water make Angistri a small paradise. If you have a boat you can sail round the island and discover its pristine little harbours. Because no cars are allowed on Angistri, hiking enthusiasts can explore the forest or walk to the more isolated beaches around the island, which are ideal for swimming and fishing.

Angistri's little paradise offers all the comforts of a modern tourist resort.

Angistri consists of three towns, Skala, Limenaria and the capital, Milos or Megalohori.

The newly-built town of **Skala**, the island's main port, is where most visitors choose to stay. It offers hotels, restaurants, bars, and the island's most-frequented beach, where water-sports equipment may be rented. The pure white Church of Agii Anargiri stands out among Skala's buildings. To the left of Skala an

View of the tourist village of Skala with the Church of Agii Anargiri

The village of Metohi, as seen from the sea

unpaved road runs to Halkiada beach.

From Skala a road leads uphill to the village of **Metohi**, which commands a splendid view of the sea and the pine forest.

Another road from Skala continue along the coast to **Milos** or **Megalohori** the island's second port. This seaside road is lined with restaurants, rooms to rent and small isolated beaches. At the

The coast from Skala to Milos is strung with little jewel-like beaches.

Milos offers rooms to rent and one of the island's developed beaches.

Church of Zoodohos Pigi a festival is held every year on the first Friday after Easter.

The road continues around on the south side of the island to the village of **Limenaria**, founded in the 17th century. The Church of Agia Kyriaki celebrates its Saint's Day on July 7 with a festival. Visitors to the area usually wind up on **Aponissos** beach, whose small tavernas serve fresh fish to weary swimmers. The picturesque scene is made complete by the sail-boats moored off **Doroussa**, the small islet opposite.

The beach at Aponissos and the little islet of Doroussa

Methana

Name

Methana is mentioned by the ancient traveller Pausanias in his *Troezeniaca* by the name *Methane*. Thucydides also mentions it – erroneously, Strabo tells us - as *Methene*. When it served as a naval base for the Ptolemies of Egypt, Methana was renamed *Arsinoe* in honour of the sister and wife of the King of Egypt.

History

Neolithic artefacts found near the summit of Mt. Helona testify to the fact that the peninsula was inhabited from the earliest times. There is evidence from the Early Helladic Era of human habitation extending all the way to Vromolimni.

Settlements dating from Late Helladic times, possibly Ionian, have been discovered in three places on the peninsula: in Vathi, in Throni and near the top of Mt. Helona. Their inhabitants were engaged mainly in seafaring. Proof of their Ionian ancestry is their worship of Apatouria (= Deceitful) Athena, who was also worshipped by the Ionians.

In the Geometric Era (1100-750 BC), Methana passed to the Dorians. The Troezenians sent 200 hoplites to the Battle of Plataea (479 BC) against the Persians, possibly in collaboration with the inhabitants of Methana (who were subjects of Argos).

During the Peloponnesian War, which spread to the area of the Argosaronic Gulf, the Athenian general Nikias occupied Methana, wresting it from Troezen, and established an Athenian garrison on the isthmus, which plundered neighbouring areas (425 BC). Upon Athens' defeat at Amphipolis and the Peace of Nikias (421 BC), Methana came once again under Spartan infuence.

In 273 BC, according to the French geologist Fouqué (1867), the Methana

The ruins of ancient Methana in Paleokastro

volcano erupted for the last time, at a short distance from Mt. Kameni, changing the morphology of the Gulf.

The eruption is described quite vividly by Pausanias in his Corinthiaca *(34,1). He tells that during the reign of Antigonus (277-240 BC) the volcano erupted and hot springs began to flow. Strabo adds that after the eruption, the area was unapproachable for days due to the great heat and the smell of sulphur.*

During Hellenistic times Methana was used by Patroclus, commander of the Egyptian fleet, as a naval base from which he launched his attacks on the Macedonian garrisons in Spetses and Hydra. It was renamed Arsinoe, became an important commercial port and remained under the rule of the Ptolemies for a century. When they left, it passed to the Romans.

The Town of Methana

The volcanic **peninsula of Methana** lies north of Troezen; it is connected to the Peloponnese by a narrow isthmus. Its area is 11.5 square kilometres, its population is 3000, and its distance from Piraeus is 28 nautical miles.

Famous from ancient times for its warm healing springs, Methana welcomes hundreds of Greek holidaymakers every year. Thus it has remained aloof from the crowds of foreign tourists, retaining the atmosphere of the Greek countryside.

The Castle of the French philhellene General Charles Nicolas Fabvier in Steno

The springs, whose temperature ranges between 28-34 °C, are of various types (sulphur, brine and acidic springs). There are springs at Vromolimni, at Agios Nikolaos (at the Pro locale), and at Agios Nikolaos Mouskas. They are suitable for dermatological, nervous, rheumatic, arthritic, gastric, etc. complaints.

Nineteen kilometres before the isthmus that links the peninsula to the Peloponnese, you will encounter **Kalloni** or **Lessia**, a seaside village well known for the flowers, citrus and other fruits cultivated there. It offers a few rooms to rent and a lovely pebble beach. At **Steno**, the narrowest point of the peninsula, 150-200 meters wide and 500 meters long, you will see fragments of the wall built by the Athenians during the Peloponnesian War, the Castle of Baron Fabvier (1782-1855) and the 15th-century Church of Agios Nikolaos.

The **town of Methana** lies along the sea in the southeastern part of the peninsula. The spa building stands at the entrance to the town; in front of it are most of the springs, with their characteristic odour of sulphur which gave the area its name of *Vromolimni* (= "Stinking Lake"). The Vromolimni springs began to be used for therapeutic purposes late in the 19th century.

Behind Vromolimni, at Throni, lie the ruins of an ancient tower.

The town's houses, of no particular architectural style, spread from the middle of town up toward the hill; rooms to rent

The spa building, where most of the healing springs are concentrated

Overall view of the town

are to be found in this area. Down along the well-constructed mole stand the souvenir shops, restaurants and cafeterias. Do not fail to sample the area's excellent sweets, among them the almond cookies (amigdalota), almond shortbread (= kourambiedes) and milk pies (= galaktomboureka). Also not to be missed are the fresh

The little green islet of Nissaki and the rocky islet of Mikro Nissaki

The picturesque village of Megalohori

fish and seafood. A great festival is held in town on the feast-day of the Holy Spirit (first Monday after Pentecost).

A favourite spot among visitors for a stroll is the little green islet of **Nissaki**, linked to the town by a causeway. On one side of the causeway is the town's marina, where luxury yachts are moored each summer alongside the tiny fishing-boats of skilled swordfish and tuna fishermen. The islet has been laid out very prettily, with narrow stone-paved streets and ex-

otic plants. On slightly higher ground off to one side is the Church of Agii Anargiri. Traces of a fortress and Spartan coins from the 4th century BC were found on the islet and at the end of the marina. Everyone winds up either in the pleasant "Nissaki" cafeteria which faces the illuminated town or on the small developed beach on the other side of the causeway. Next to Nissaki is the rocky islet **Mikro Nissaki**.

In addition to the one on Nissaki, there

The little fishing village of Vathi has been evolving in recent years into a tourist resort.

Paleokastro beach in Vathi

Grapevines are a unique way to decorate a house!

are other good beaches at Karastamati and **Agios Nikolaos** (at the Pro locale), where remains of ancient baths and a palace were found. The springs here began to be exploited in 1870.

Methana - Vathi - Kameni Hora

Two roads begin from town and lead in opposite directions; these are the two basic routes that you may take. One runs up to **Ano Methana**, nestled in among groves of fig-trees, olives and vineyards. Just before Vathi, you will see, on the tip of a narrow spit of land, the small chapel of Krassopanagia.

Legend has it that it was built with water and wine by a wine merchant who narrowly escaped drowning nearby!

The road passes through **Megalohori**, a picturesque little village with red-tiled roofs, flower-filled gardens and olive presses. In the village's narrow streets you will encounter more donkeys than

The most enchanting area of Methana, "troubled" Kameni Hora

The Church of Agia Varvara

The tiny hamlet of Kato Mouska

cars. Another road leads up to the equally picturesque village of **Megalopotami**.

You will end up in **Vathi**, the port of Megalohori; it is a small fishing village which has recently begun evolving into a tourist resort. You can find accommodation in rented rooms and sample the freshly-caught fish in the village's little tavernas. Another road leads to the Paleokastro site. The pebbles on the shore are testimony to the volcanic composition of the soil. The area offers a few rooms to rent.

Walking along the beach, you come to the "Paleokastro" taverna. Rising behind it are the ruins of the acropolis and the walls of ancient Methana dating from 425 BC. Also discovered here were the ruins of a temple of Apollo. The ancient city lies under the sea opposite the beach.

You turn around and drive through pine-clad hills towards **Kameni Hora**, perhaps the loveliest area on the Methana peninsula, with a few rooms to rent. It is a small village whose picturesque white houses are decked out with grapevines. In among them are large reddish-black volcanic rocks, which rolled down when the crater, looming just over the village, spewed them out with disastrous results. The coast is indented with small harbours, ideal for swimming and fishing, but accessible only by boat. Across the water can be seen the shores of the Peloponnese and the chapel of Krassopanagia.

Those who wish may leave their car in Kameni Hora and follow the signs to the top of Mt. Kameni at an elevation of 417 m to see the area's biggest crater, 150 m in circumference and 60 m deep. Be sure to take some water along, and choose a cool time of day, either early in the morning or late in the evening, when you will also be rewarded with a stunning sunset. The climb takes about 20 minutes.

Methana - Palea Loutra

If you set out in the opposite direction from that of the previous route, you will come to the lovely beach of Limnionas, where there is a discotheque. Take the way up to **Kipseli**, built on volcanic soil. Just opposite, the village of Perdika on Aegina can be discerned, along with the rocky islet of Petrokaravo, perilous for ships. You will reach **Agii Theodori**, a small village with old houses. Now head for Kounoupitsa and the lovely stone Church of Agia Varvara.

It is said that the bones of Saint Barbara are in the church's basement, and that if one presses a coin to her icon and it stays there, any wish he makes will come true!

Three kilometres further along, you will come to **Kounoupitsa**, where there was a school of rug-making until 1989. In the Church of the Panagia, dedicated to the Presentation of the Virgin, a festival is held on August 23. From there continue

The Church of the Panagia in Kounoupitsa

The seaside Church of Agios Georgios

on towards **Palea Loutra (Kato Mouska)**, a picturesque village on a pine-blanketed hill with a stunning view of Angistri. At the top of the hill you will see the Church of the Assumption of the Virgin dating from 1859. Just above it is **Makrilongos (Apano Mouska)**, with a view in the direction of Agios Georgios.

The road descends to the seaside fishing village of **Agios Georgios**, with country homes and the Church of Agios Georgios, which celebrates its Saint's day

The village of Agios Georgios, seen from Apano Mouska

on April 23 with a festival. The road winds up in the seaside town of **Agios Nikolaos Mouskas**, site of the springs of the same name. They were fist mentioned by Pausanias, who believed they were created when the Kameni volcano erupted in the 3rd century BC. There are Roman walls in the area, and there may have been a reservoir for baths.

On the north coast of the peninsula (here the shore at Agios Nikolaos), rocks of solidified lava are testimony to the disaster in 283 BC.

Poros

Name

The word Poros is a geographical term meaning a narrow strip of sea linking two small bays, i.e. a strait or a sea passage. Indeed, the distance between Poros and the shore opposite is at its narrowest point only 200 m.

Ancient authors first mentioned Poros by the name of *Eirene* (= peace), perhaps an allusion to the peace which prevailed in the area after the Dorian invasion and the breakdown of the Mycenean state (Geometric Era, 9th-8th centuries BC).

Poros is made up of two islands, Sphaeria and Calauria, originating in two different geological periods. Sphaeria owed its name to Sphaerus, who was buried on the island. Later it was renamed *Hiera* (= sacred) by Aethra, daughter of the wise King of Troezen Pittheus, because Aethra had founded a temple dedicated to Deceitful Athena, and celebrations were held here in her honour.

The other island was known as Scelerdia and took on the name of Calauria when the city was built around the sanctuary. Calauria means fair breeze, and may allude to the favourable winds which the god offers to seafarers. (Such a mild breeze blows during the summer months even today – the island is generally free from strong winds). But perhaps it received that name from "Calauropian" Apollo (a pastoral god who carried a shepherd's crook); he had been worshipped formerly on the island.

Mythology

In his description of the temple of Poseidon, Pausanias tells how Poseidon gave Apollo his place at the Delphic oracle and in Delos in exchange for Cape Taenaron and Calauria.

Sphaerus or Myrtilus, son of Hermes and a skilful charioteer, helped Pelops

The islands of Calauria and Sphaeria. In the centre is the narrow isthmus that connects them.

win the chariot race with the crafty king of Pissa Oenomaus and marry his daughter Hippodameia. One version of the myth relates that Pelops killed Sphaerus immediately after his victory, another that he killed him when he tried to kiss Hippodameia, and a third that Hippodameia fell in love with Sphaerus and when he rejected her advances she accused him of rape to Pelops.

As far as neighbouring Troezen is concerned, the myth relates that the matricide Orestes came here to be purified of the murders he had committed. The philosopher and writer Plutarch (AD 50-120) tells us that this was the birthplace of Theseus, the national hero of the ancient Greeks, the Ionians in particular. His mother was Aethra and his father either the King of Athens, Aegeus, or, if Pausanias is to be believed, Poseidon.

The usual version of the myth tells how wise Pittheus got his guest, Aegeus, drunk and helped him into bed with his daughter Aethra. Pausanias' version says that Athena appeared to Aethra that same night in her sleep and ordered her to go to Sphaeria and make a sacrifice on the grave of Sphaerus. Poseidon was waiting for her there, and she also lay with him. Aethra founded a temple in honour of Deceitful Athena, where the virgins of Troezen dedicated their maidenly girdles before they were married.

One myth has it that when Theseus

was seven years old, Heracles stayed as a guest in Pittheus' palace. The other boys ran away when they spied Heracles' lion-skin, but Theseus armed himself with an axe, believing he had to deal with a real lion! At the age of 16 he managed to move the huge rock under which Aegeus had hidden a sword and a pair of sandals, whereupon he set out to find his father in Athens. He did not take the sea route, which would have been safer, but travelled over the highroads, where he performed several of his labours.

When Theseus helped Heracles defeat the Amazons and take the magic girdle of their Queen, Hippolyte, Heracles rewarded him by giving him the Amazon Antiope, daughter of Ares in marriage. By her Theseus had a son, Hippolytus. According to Plutarch, after his wife was killed fighting at his side in the battle with the Amazons, he decided to marry Phaedra, daughter of Minos, and sent his son to his great-grandfather Pittheus in Troezen.

Scattered columns from the temple of Poseidon

Pausanias relates that Theseus, now married to Phaedra, returned to Troezen to be purified of the murder of his uncle Pallas. Diodorus the Sicilian tells that Phaedra fell madly in love with Hippolytus and when he rejected her she calumniated him to his father. Theseus asked Poseidon to make an example of Hippolytus, and when he was killed, Phaedra committed suicide.

There are two versions of his death, according to Pausanias: either he was killed when Poseidon overturned his chariot and was resurrected by Aesculapius, or he ascended into the heavens and became the well-known constellation. As for Theseus, a wave of popular indignation forced him to leave the land, and he was killed on Skyros by King Lycomedes. After the Persian Wars, the Athenians, on the instructions of the oracle at Delphi, brought his bones to Athens and did him the appropriate honours.

Cape Scyllaeus (present-day Tselevinia) is said to have taken its name from the mythical princess Scylla who killed her father, the King of Megara, by cutting off his magic lock of purple hair to please the King of Crete, Minos. The myth tells that on the way back from Crete, Minos, who had promised to marry her, threw her in the sea and she was washed up on Scyllaeus, or that her dead father, transformed into an eagle, strangled her. No one would bury the body of the treacherous daughter, and her spirit still stirs up tempests to torment passing ships!

History

The Dryopians were present in limited numbers in Poros around the end of the Late Helladic Era (13th century BC), occupying the site where the town was to grow up later around the temple of Poseidon.

One powerful Mycenean naval station in the area was the precipitous rocky islet

Modi or Liontari, on the east coast of Poros; it may have been the base of the powerful Heionians or the precursor of Poros' Amphictyony of Calauria.

The Troezenians took part in the Trojan War. During the Geometric Era, Troezen passed to the Dorians. As for the Calaurians, they remained subjects of Troezen throughout the Archaic Era. The harbour of Pogon served both areas, which in the centuries to come were to follow the same historical course.

In the mid-7th century the Amphictyony of Calauria came onto the scene; its seat was the temple of Calaurian Poseidon, which had existed on Poros since the end of the 8th century BC. It was a naval, religious and political federation which numbered among its members Athens, Aegina, Epidaurus, Hermione, Nauplia, Prasiae and Orchomenus. They banded together to defend their independence and their commerce from the Argives. When the Argive leader Pheidon conquered Nauplia, he was allowed to join the Amphictyony, and, as finds from the temple show, it then acquired great power (Strabo VII, 374). This heyday lasted until 459 BC, and during that period great public buildings and sanctuaries were built. The Amphictyony started to lose its peculiar tribal character (Dryopian) when Sparta occupied Prasiae and became a member. It continued in existence, however, until the 3rd century BC.

At the beginning of the 5th century BC, the Persian fleet sailed into the Aegean. In the spring of 480 BC the Persians attempted to attack Greece for the second time. The Troezenians sent five ships to the Battle of Artemisium in Evia and helped fortify the isthmus of Corinth. The women and children of Athens took refuge in Troezen (ballot of Themistocles). United, the Greeks assembled their naval forces at Salamis. They also sent 2000 hoplites to Plataea, possibly in collaboration with the inhabitants of Methana (479 BC).

When the two most powerful cities of the Greek world, Athens and Sparta, decided to vie for supremacy, the terrible Peloponnesian War broke out, and quickly spread to include the area of the Argosaronic Gulf. The Troezenians allied themselves with the Spartans and in 430 BC Athens sacked Troezen.

When the Macedonians appeared in the Greek world in the mid-4th century BC, the Greek cities opposed them, and Troezen provided refuge for Athenogenes, an anti-Macedonian Athenian, who became tyrant of the area. As for that other uncompromising Athenian, the orator Demosthenes, he sought asylum in 322 BC in the temple of Poseidon in Calauria, but as he was still in danger of being apprehended, he committed suicide by drinking poison.

Demosthenes, famous for his moral courage and self-discipline, overcame two physical handicaps and became a famous orator. To overcome his lisp, he filled his mouth with pebbles and recited verse. As for his shyness, he orated at the seashore, particularly when the sea

"Themistocles' ballot" was a vote in the Athenian boule on evacuation of the city (Museum of Inscriptions).

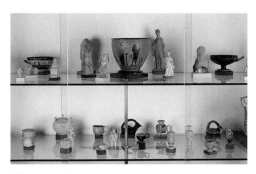

Clay pots, figurines and jewellery from ancient Troezen (Poros Museum)

was stormy, to become accustomed to the roar of a crowd. In his *Life of Demosthenes*, Plutarch tells us that when the treasurer Arpalus embezzled 5000 talents from the fortune of Alexander the Great, he sought refuge as a beggar in Athens. Although in the beginning Demosthenes was in favour of turning him away, in the end he proposed that the Athenians take him in. When Arpalus stole a large sum from the Acropolis and made off with it, the Athenians accused Demosthenes of having been bribed by Arpalus. Unable to repay the stolen treasure, he escaped from prison and sought refuge first in Aegina and then in Troezen. In the summer of 323 BC, when Alexander died, he returned in triumph to Athens. The following year, however, the Macedonians defeated the Athenians in the Battle of Lamia, and Demosthenes sought asylum in the temple of Poseidon. When he was

View from inside one of the upper stories of the Tower of Damalas, built on the ruins of the Hellenistic fortress of ancient Troezen.

asked to give himself up, he preferred to commit suicide by drinking the poison he had hidden either in his pen or his ring. Before he died he managed to drag himself away from the temple, to keep from desecrating the sacred place.

Basing himself on letters sent by the Macedonian commander to Rhodes in which he named all those who had been bribed by Arpalus, Pausanias cast doubt on Demosthenes' guilt: his name was not mentioned, even though he had been opposed to the Macedonians.

In 273 BC, the Methana volcano erupted for the last time – as described by Pausanias in his *Corinthiaca* – and changed the morphology of the Gulf. Sphaeria was cut off from Methana, and together with Calauria formed what is today Poros.

During the Roman occupation, Calauria was once again in the possession of Troezen. It was repeatedly attacked by pirates during that time. Early in the 1st century, the ambitious King of Pontus Mithridates VI, son of Eupator, allied himself with Cilician and Cretan pirates and clashed with the Romans, inciting the Greeks to rebel. Mithridates was curbed by the Roman proconsul Leucius Cornelius Sulla in 86 BC. After the defeat of their allies, the Cilician pirates plundered the islands and coastal areas, sacking cities and temples, among them Poseidon's in Calauria. In AD 396, the Goths added to the destruction, which was made complete a short time later by a severe earthquake.

During the reign of the Byzantine emperor Leon VI the Wise (AD 866-912), Troezen was renamed *Damalas* after a wealthy official who had large land holdings in the area. When the Franks occupied Corinth (1204), Damalas fell into their hands. During that whole period the island of Poros remained essentially uninhabited, as the whole north coast served as a base of operations for Berber pirates until 1382.

After the fall of Constantinople to the Turks in 1453, the Greeks ceded the three castles of the Argolid to the Venetians; among them was the castle of Damalas, which remained in Venetian hands until 1531.

During the Turkish occupation Poros assembled a great commercial fleet, but it never gained the reputation of Hydra and Spetses' fleets because it did not become active in battle as theirs did. In 1463 Poros received Arvanite refugees from the Peloponnese. A second wave of Arvanites took refuge on Poros around 1540. The island played quite a significant role, however, during the 1821 Revolution, as its proximity to the Peloponnese made it a stopping- and meeting-place for famous leaders of the times, despite the fact that Turkish troops were garrisoned on the coast opposite. During the Russo-Turkish War of 1806-1812, the Russians built their naval station with the islanders' help.

After independence, the island was used several times as a provisional seat of the anti-government committee of the free Greek state. The governor Kapodistrias stayed on the island from April until June, 1827, when he relocated in Nauplio.

In 1828 work began on the first Greek naval station (near the present-day Gymnasium-Lyceum), which remained there until 1878. In September 1828 the ambassadors of the three Great Powers met in Poros before conferring with Kapodistrias on setting the boundaries of the new Greek state.

In July 1831 tragic incidents took place in the port of Poros; protagonists were the naval commanders who had brought glory to the Greek fleet. The naval officers from Hydra and Mani, who were opposed to the Kapodistrias government, sent ships under the command of the Hydraean Admiral Andreas Miaoulis to defeat the national fleet. The outcome of the civil conflict was that the best ships

Local costume of Poros-Hydra from the book by Stackelberg "La Grèce, Vues pittoresques et topographiques", *Paris 1834,* (Athanassiou collection).

in the Greek fleet were taken over: the steamship "Karteria", the corvettes and "Emmanouella" and "Hydra" and the frigate "Ellas". The two latter were blown up on August 1/13. This was the beginning of the opposition to Kapodistrias, which led to his assassination that same year.

Poros can boast that it has been a source of inspiration for many famous artists of this century, both Greek and foreign. The poet George Seferis, recipient

Narrow lanes and stairs lead up to Roloi.

of the Nobel Prize in Literature, wrote a series of poems here, one of which is *"Kihli"*. The author Kosmas Politis wrote his *"Lemonodassos"* here. The essay-writer Dr. Angelos Tanagras perfected his metaphysical meditations in his book *"Poros – Islets of the Saronic Gulf – Philosophical Walks"*. The hagiographer Giorgos Parthenis painted the fresco of the Pantocrator in the Church of Agios Georgios. The well-known American author Henry Miller described the island in his famous *"Colossus of Maroussi"*.

The Town of Poros

Poros has an area of 31.3 square kilometres and a population of approximately 4,000; it lies at a distance of 32 nautical miles from Piraeus.

The town is built amphitheatrically on the two rocky hills of a three-cornered islet, Sphaeria; it has been declared a na-

View of the town of Poros. Inset: engraving of "Calauria and Galatas" from a book by Worlthsworth written in 1839 (Athanassiou collection).

Elaborate workmanship in the town's wrought-iron balcony railings

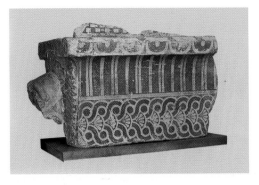

A decorated clay sime from the Archaic temple of Aphrodite Acraea (Poros Museum)

tional landmark, protected by law from unseemly development. Its houses, lacking any particular architectural plan, are stacked one on top of the other, and are roofed with terra cotta tiles. They have brightly-painted facades and classical-style external elements (ornamental tiles at the edges of the roofs, decorative bands, plaster bas-reliefs, and wrought-iron railings on the balconies).

The town's first houses were built in the Kasteli quarter by Arvanites from the Peloponnese who moved here in 1463 to escape Turkish persecution. The view from here is breathtaking. On the top of the second hill is a ruined mill and the Chapel of Agios Athanassios.

The small but interesting Archaeological Museum of Poros stands in Korizis Square (opening hours 8:30 am-3:00 pm daily, closed Mondays). Its exhibits include finds from ancient Calauria and

Troezen. Also worth visiting are the 19th-century Church of Evangelistria and Agios Konstantinos, and Agios Georgios (1861), whose frescos were painted by the hagiographers Theotokis and Parthenis.

Most visitors get around Sphaeria on the island's circular road. The small uninhabited rocky islet of Bourtzi can be seen jutting out of the narrow strip of water between Poros and Galatas. It has walls of a fortress built in 1827 on the urging of King Otho's philhellene Viceroy, Heideck. The tour of the island ends at the bridge connecting Sphaeria to the main island of Calauria.

Poros has a well-developed tourist infrastructure. Visitors will easily find accommodation in modern hotels and rooms to rent in homes. Possibilities for entertainment, eating and drinking vary from cinemas, bars and discos to restaurants boasting international cuisine and

The chapel of Agios Athanassios blesses the town of Poros.

The uninhabited rocky islet of Bourtzi

In observation of Nautical Week

Poros' little tavernas guarantee unique gastronom-ic delights.

small tavernas serving wine out of the barrel accompanied by grilled octopus. At patisseries, ask to sample the island's bottled lemonade and almond cookies (= amigdalota). Poros' waterfront, the centre of island life, presents a lively, pleasant sight, with anchors and cannon, souvenir shops, colourful tablecloths in its bustling restaurants and little fishing boats, nets spread out on their decks, rubbing shoulders with luxury yachts. Excursion boats depart from here to Epidaurus, Nauplio (and Mycenae), and the other islands of the Argosaronic Gulf.

One event no one should miss is Nautical Week, celebrated each summer; it includes games, artistic events and exhibitions. For 15 days each summer an exact copy of an ancient trireme (5th-century BC warship) manned by an international crew is moored in what its designer, Professor Morrison, calls the "sheltered" waters of Poros.

Poros - Neoria

The islands of Sphaeria and Calauria were once connected by a low-lying sandy isthmus, in which a narrow channel 125 m long and 4.8 m wide was dug in

During the summer months the harbour overflows with luxury craft.

The vast beach on the Isthmus

1877. This is the site of the Centre for Recruit Training of the Greek Navy, which is housed in the premises of the first Russian Naval Station of 1806. In the Centre's courtyard stands the obelisk/tomb of the captain of the S/S "Karteria" Lord Hastings.

Whereas Sphaeria is a dry rock of volcanic origin, **Calauria** is verdant with pine, olive and lemon-trees, with plenty of water. The shore between **Mikro Neorio** and **Megalo Neorio** is indented with spacious

The gate of the Centre for Recruit Training of the Greek Navy

sandy inlets where the sea is tranquil and the pine-trees and tamarisks often extend right down to the edge of the sea. The loveliest of these sandy coves is the "Limanaki tis Agapis" (= Harbour of Love).

Just beyond the Aspros Gatos region,

The Church of the Evangelistria on the waterfront

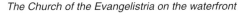

In the "Harbour of Love" the water takes on a green colour from the pine forest on the shore.

you will see the Villa Galini, where Henry Miller stayed in 1938, and George Seferis was a guest in 1946. Here sports enthusiasts can find all the equipment they need for water-skiing, windsurfing, sailing, etc. Both Mikro Neorio and Megalo Neorio offer schools of windsurfing and water-skiing. The sea off the island's shores abounds in Blackfish.

A short distance beyond Megalo Neorio you will see the ruins of the Russian

Naval Station, on the site where it was moved in 1834-6. Offshore lies the islet of **Daskalio** with the small Church of the Assumption of the Virgin.

Poros - Askeli - Monastery of Zoodohos Pigi of Calauria

Another route beginning at the bridge

Famous men of letters of our century were guests in Villa Galini (owned by Dragoumis).

The naval station was first built by the Russians in 1806; it was destroyed in the civil conflict of 1831 and was later moved here where it remained until 1836.

leads to **Askeli**, a pine-clad seaside village, about 3 km northeast of Poros. The area offers modern hotel complexes, bars and restaurants, as well as superb beaches, of both the sand and pebble variety. At the mouth of the bay stands the small white Church of the Assumption.

This way to the **Monastery of Zoodohos Pigi of Calauria** was the Greek poet Seferis' favourite walk. The monastery can be reached either by local bus, or by caique from Poros. The pure white monastery, an outstanding example of island monastic architecture, is situated in the thickly forested Monastiri locale, commanding a panoramic view of the sea and the coast of the Peloponnese opposite.

Just before the monastery you will encounter the small Church of Agii Anargiri with its fine carved wooden altar-screen. Nearby is a picturesque coffee shop with outdoor tables where visitors can admire the stately plane-trees growing in the gorge below. Among their roots flows spring-water, now reduced to a trickle. This is the same water said to have cured the Metropolitan of Athens, Iakovos II, of gall-stones, inspiring him to found the monastery in the mid-1700s. This spring, whose water is "undying" according to popular tradition, has also given the

The small Church of the Assumption of the Virgin on Daskalio islet

monastery its name (zoodohos pigi = life-giving spring)!

Although on the outside it has the look of a fortress, with windows and loop-holes on the ground floor, on the inside peace

Between Mikro and Megalo Neorio is a string of small organised sand beaches, suitable for water-sports.

The little Church of Agii Anargiri

ing smaller church dedicated to the Taxi-arhes.

Inside the church you will see the priceless wooden altar-screen, said to have been carved in Cappadocia in Asia Minor in the 17th century, along with important icons, like the one painted by Raphael Ceccoli (1853) which portrays the Virgin holding the infant Jesus. The monastery is open to visitors daily from 8:00 am to 2:00 pm and from 4:00 pm to 8:00 pm. Every year on the first Friday after Easter, the monastery celebrates with a grand festival, at which time many pilgrims find accommodation in its hospice.

Because it enjoyed protection and many privileges under Turkish rule, the monastery became a meeting-place for Greek Revolutionaries, and many naval fighters in the 1821 War of Independence asked to be buried here. One tradition says that the mortal remains of Demosthenes were also moved here. During the German occupation it served as a hiding-place for Greeks being helped to escape

and simplicity reign. In the middle of its entranceway stand a sturdy bell-tower and two immense cypress-trees.

The monastery church dominates the centre of the courtyard. It is a domed basilica, erected on the site of a pre-exist-

Modern hotels and restaurants beckon visitors to the village of Askeli.

The beach near the Monastery

Venerable priests will show you around the mona-stery

to the Middle East. One story goes that once when the Germans were rounding up resistance fighters, some of them hid in the thick foliage of the 35-meter-high cypress trees in the courtyard! The monastery has also been instrumental in raising the cultural level of the islanders.

Below the monastery, you can swim at the developed beach and be instructed in the schools of windsurfing and water-ski-ing. For lunch, sample a few traditional dishes in the area's small tavernas.

Poros - Sanctuary of Calaurian Poseidon

The area around the sanctuary was al-ready inhabited in the Geometric Era. The

The famous Monastery of Zoodohos Pigi of Calauria

ancient city was built on the slopes of Mt. Profitis Ilias and extended down to the Bay of Vagiona. It was during this era that Poseidon began to be worshipped at his sanctuary here. The mid 7th century BC saw the founding of the Amphictyony of Calauria, with the sanctuary as its headquarters. When Argos joined the Amphictyony, the sanctuary acquired great power and held it until 459 BC. It continued in use up to the 3rd century BC.

The Doric **temple of Calaurian Poseidon** was built on an elevated stretch of level ground around 520 BC. Constructed of Aeginetan porous stone and trachyte, it stood in a rectangular enclosure and had two entrances. It was a peripteral hexastyle with 12 columns on the flanks. In the Classical Era a larger shrine, extending out to the southwest, was established around the old temple. Around 420 BC a limestone stoa was built on the northwest side of the shrine and 50 years later another stoa was added,

Delegates met in the temple of Poseidon, which lies nestled in a pine forest.

an extension of the first. In 350 BC a third limestone stoa was added, this one branching off at an angle. Finally, around 320 BC a fourth stoa was built (an extension of the third) of limestone and porous stone. Construction came to an end in Hellenistic times, after the priests' quarters and a propylon were built between the stoas. Archaeologists have not yet located Demosthenes' grave, which Pausanias noted inside the temple enclosure.

The area ceased to be inhabited in AD 395, under the emperor Arcadius, when Goths led by Alaric invaded and laid waste a large portion of the Peloponnese. Anything left standing was demolished by a severe earthquake a short time later. This is when the ancient town of Calauria at Vagionia is believed to have been engulfed by the sea. When the water is calm, ruins of buildings can still be seen.

Excavations on the site were initiated in 1894 by the Swedish archaeologists S. Wide and L. Kjellberg, and were continued by the archaeologist G. Welter up to 1938. But natural and humanly caused disasters – after 1760 ships from Hydra began to carry hewn stone of all types from the temple back to Hydra, where it was used in building and decorating that island's famous mansions – have made it very difficult to complete the investigations and form an integrated picture of the site that visitors see today. The area is, however, worth visiting, if only for the marvellous view it affords of the sea, Methana and the Peloponnesian coast; on a clear day Attica and Salamina can be seen!

From the temple, a road runs down to the Bay of **Vagionia**, with a few houses, a small jetty where boats tie up and a small sandy beach. During the period of Frankish rule, the gulf became a base of operations for Berber pirates, and it is still known as *Barbaria* today.

Poros - Galatas - Trizina

You can take one of the frequent ferries or other boats across from Poros to the coast of **Galatas**. The distance between them is only 200 m at their closest point; according to Pausanias, it was once possible to walk across to Troezen! The area offers modern tourist accommodations, restaurants and tavernas. There is also an organised campsite.

Most visitors want to make the short trip to the well-known **Lemonodassos**, a vast orchard east of Galatas planted with 30,000 lemon- and orange-trees, site of a number of water-mills. You can swim at Lemonodassos beach or walk to the nearby beach at Aliki. And, like everyone else, you will probably wind up at the taverna on the top of the hill next to the waterfall that provides the water used to irrigate the lemon forest. Other beaches, just as fine, are those at Agia Anna, Plaka and Artimos.

About 9 kilometres west of Galatas, the road turns up away from the sea, toward the village of **Trizina (Damalas)**. Just about one kilometre outside the village, between two torrent-beds below Trizina's lemon orchard, lie the ruins of ancient Troezen. Also known as Poseidonia, it was one of the most ancient cult centres of Poseidon. It was named Troezen,

Quaint tavernas in Galatas with a view of Poros

however, after Pelops' son.

Excavations of the site were first carried out by the French School of Archaeology in 1890 and 1899, and later, in 1932, by the German Archaeological Institute. On the top of the hill stood the acropolis, site of the temple of Athena of Strength. The city was surrounded by a brick wall, of which nothing remains. Of the dividing wall added in Hellenistic times between the main city and its outlying districts, only two square towers and the ground floor of another larger one, today known as the *palace of Theseus*, have survived. The tower was restored in the Middle Ages by the Frankish governor

The shore of Galatas seen from Poros

The tower of Damalas or "Palace of Theseus"

of the area.

Outside the city was a temple of Poseidon of Growth, which the Troezenians built to propitiate the god's wrath.

Myth has it that when Althepus was king, Poseidon and Athena quarrelled over who was to be protector of the Argolid. When Athena came to rule the area, Poseidon dried up all the springs and flooded the fields of the Argolid with seawater. Finally Zeus intervened and made them both protectors of the area, and thus Poseidon and Athena shared the acropolis of Troezen.

Near the temple of Poseidon there was a thesmophorium (= temple dedicated to Demeter), where many figurines and other artefacts were found. The grey boulder called the *rock of Theseus* is said to be the rock under which his father hid his sword and sandals. On the spot where the sanctuary of Bridal Aphrodite is believed to have stood, there is today a small white church.

The temple of Hippolytus was founded in the 4th century BC, and it is Troezen's most ancient temple. It is said to have housed the tomb of Hippolytus, but it would appear that the deity originally worshipped there was later identified with the hero. Outside the temple was an altar and behind it a stoa. The temple was destroyed in the earthquakes that accompanied the eruption of the Methana volcano. It was peripteral and amphiprostyle (6x11

Very few ruins remain of ancient Troezen.

columns). Around the 3rd century BC an Aesculapium and an Enkoimitirion (= infirmary) were established north of the temple, because Hippolytus was believed to have the ability to heal. To the east of Hippolytus' shrine were the stadium, gymnasium and agora (near the Church of Agios Georgios), and a little further on the ancient theatre and stoa. The rest of the city's sanctuaries stood here; their building materials were later used to construct neighbouring churches.

One such obvious case is that of the Byzantine Church of Panagia Episkopi, built on the ruins of an Byzantine basilica of the 8th century AD out of material from the temple of Peeping Aphrodite. It was built in stages, as the stonework in the walls and other technical indications would suggest. Still visible are the main church, the narthex, sanctum, exonarthex and the ante-rooms.

Also worth visiting is the newly-built Monastery of Keharitomeni in the Agios Panteleimon locale, 3 km east of Trizina.

Behind the Tower of Damalas is Diavologefiro (Devil's Bridge), an enchanting place, ideal for a picnic.

The medieval Church of Panagia Episkopi.

Hydra

Name

Hydra has retained its Mycenean name of *Hydrea*, indicative of the many springs the island had at that time, making it a suitable place for Dryopian shepherds to settle. The island's Orthodox Greek and Arvanite inhabitants used the name Hydrea up to the 18th century. Another ancient name which has come down to us is that of Hydra's highest peak, Ere, which means land as a mountain massif.

History

Human presence on Hydra was intermittent, as proved by the single potsherd from the Late Neolithic Era (3000-2600 BC) discovered in the Bay of Agios Georgios. Sites of early Helladic settlements which served as way-stations between the Peloponnese and the Cyclades have also been discovered on Hydra and Dokos.

During the Late Helladic Era (13th century BC), Hydrea became an outpost of the kingdom of Mycenae because its land was suitable for supporting the mountain-dwelling Dryopians, stock-breeders of those times. During the following centuries the island's few inhabitants are not of special historical interest. Around the end of the Mycenean Era (about 1170 BC), Hydrea was attacked by the Myceneans.

The ancient historian Herodotus tells us that (III, 57) that Hydrea was sold by the Hermioneans around 528/526 BC to Samian oligarchic fugitives, who had unsuccessfully attempted to overthrow the tyrant Polycrates. The Samians departed for Cydonia in Crete (present-day Hania), when mighty Aegina retaliated against their pirate raids. They ceded Hydrea to the Troezenians, who held it, using it as grazing land, until the 4th century BC.

During the Persian Wars, the Hydraeans may have taken part in the historic Battle of Salamis. The island took the side of Sparta in the Peloponnesian War.

When the Macedonians appeared on the scene, Hydrea once again served as a naval base and grazing land, this time for the powerful city of Halieis, but when the latter was invaded and destroyed, Hydrea fell into obscurity along with it. In 167 BC Greece became a Roman province; repeated pirate raids devastated her coastal areas. This was why the geographer Strabo did not consider the islands of the Argosaronic Gulf worth mentioning.

After the Byzantine Empire was split in two in 1204, Hydra was ruled by the Venetians until it passed to the Turks in 1460. Ravaged by their attacks, it was resettled by Greek and Arvanite refugees from the Peloponnese (1470). Due to its barren soil, they earned a living as fishermen and sailors. A second wave of Arvanites took refuge in Hydra in 1540.

During the first Russo-Turkish War of 1768-1774, Hydra took part in the Orloff events. When the Küçük Kaynarca Treaty was signed in 1774, the Hydraean fleet gained the privilege of sailing under protection of the Russian flag. The island remained almost independent; it was self-administered by elders and Turkish representatives appointed by the Hydraeans themselves. A period of economic development followed, brought about mainly by shipping and commerce, particularly with the outbreak of the Napoleonic Wars. Hydraeans became fabulously wealthy. The island was often referred to as *Little England* and at the end of the Turkish occupation it had the first merchant navy school in Europe, as well as other schools, where famous Greek men of letters such as A. Efessios, N. Vamvas, A. Gazis and T. Farmakidis were employed as teachers. In 1807, after a promise by the Russian Admiral Siniavin, the Hydraeans again revolted against the Turks.

Fresco of Hydra, painted by Pavlos Pantelakis (based on engravings dating from 1796).

When the Revolution broke out, Greek leaders from the Peloponnese wrote to the Hydraeans asking them to join them in the struggle. After a few objections on the part of the elders, the islanders, urged on by the sea-captain Antonios Ikonomou, resolved to take part in the revolution. Through the efforts of Hatzigiannis Mexis, a leader from Spetses, Hydra soon joined the struggle, with about 100 ships!

In addition to their glorious historical memories, Hydraeans also recollect the ugly sides of the Greek War of Independence. When, after the Second National

The bronze statue of A. Miaoulis

Assembly in Astros, civil war broke out between the chieftains and the oligarchs, the son of the Revolutionary hero Theodoros Kolokotronis was murdered in Nauplio. On February 6, 1825 the governor Ioannis Koletis and the executive and its president G. Kountouriotis imprisoned the leaders of the "party of trouble-makers and malefactors" in the Monastery of Profitis Ilias; among them was Kolokotronis himself! They were released on May 16, when the danger of Ibrahim Pasha loomed close.

In 1825, machinery was donated by the French publisher and philhellene Firmin Didot, and the island's first printing office was set up. The newspapers *"Friend of the Law"* and *"Apoikoi greci"* were published by the Italian professor in Hydra Giuseppe Chiappe.

After the Turkish yoke was thrown off, the Hydraeans never regained the fortunes they had spent in the Struggle. They began earn their living as spongefishers and sailors, but gradually the island went into decline, its population dwindled and the centre of commerce shifted to Siros and Piraeus. Hydra continued, however, to provide Greece with famous men after she won her freedom from the Turks. Among them were Admiral Pavlos Kountouriotis (1855-1935), hero of the Balkan Wars, who was elected Greece's first President in 1924, and Dimitrios Voulgaris (1802-1877), elected Prime Minister of Greece in 1855. Hydra also produced famous men of the arts and letters who made great contributions to the island's cultural development;

among them were the artists N. Hatzikiriakos-Gikas, P. Tetsis, N. Nikolaou, etc.

During World War II, the Italian and German occupation forces left the island in shambles. In the post-War years, Greek and foreign films made on the island (*Marina, The Girl in Black, The Boy and the Dolphin, Phaedra*, etc.) made it one of the most important gathering-places in Europe for the jet-set. Today Hydra's main source of income is tourism.

The Town of Hydra

Hydra has an area of 56 square kilometres and a population of 2,373. It lies 37 nautical miles from Piraeus.

A living monument to a particularly charming cultural tradition, with a cosmopolitan atmosphere and dynamic night-life, the Hydra of Seferis, Engonopoulos, Miller, Elytis and Doxiadis has become a centre of meditation and artistic creation. The marvel of its stern architectural style has inspired many artists to create masterpieces and Hydra has come to be a pole of attraction and a place of residence for intellectuals. It has become synonymous with high society and a showy display of wealth and power, just as in the past it paraded the riches brought home by its fleet.

Hydra is an ideal venue for high-scale tourism. Its excellent yacht supply depots and facilities of every kind have made Hydra's port a favourite among Greek ship-owners. Luxury yachts, fishing boats and colourful crowds continually bustle in and out of its busy harbour. A tanker brings the island its water from Poros every day.

The Square and statue of P. Kountouriotis on Hydra's waterfront by night

In addition to Hydra's main market, there are always fishermen selling straight from their boats!

When some fête is under way, the water-tanker drops anchor in the harbour and serves as a stage! Greece's last barge, the "Eleni", loaded with goods of every kind, from building materials to foodstuffs, sets out from Piraeus and sails into Hydra's port, where the island's 500 or so donkeys are waiting to carry them up the hill.

Narrow streets and staircases lead up to the Kiafa quarter.

The old ships' cannon in the square – on the site of the harbour's eastern fortress – still stand guard over the historic port and town. In the centre stands the bronze statue of Admiral A. Miaoulis (1769-1835). Below this square the road to Mandraki begins. Here, too, are cannon and the bronze bust of the Prime Minister Admiral Antonios Kriezis (1796-1865).

The area was already inhabited in Mycenean times, as shown by the few potsherds and flakes of obsidian found in the surrounding hills, since every other trace of ancient or medieval habitation was covered when the town was built up in the 17th-century. Narrow lanes and staircases lead up to Kiafa, the island's first organised 17th century settlement. Its inhabitants, unable to tame the barren land, turned, timidly at first, towards the sea; in a short time they had become masters of the Aegean and contenders for naval supremacy in the Mediterranean. Local master-builders and their guilds were in demand all over Greece; here they built magnificent flat-roofed stone houses.

From 1700 on, trade in the Mediterranean was no longer limited to commercial transactions, but expanded to include cultural exchanges. Grey stone mansions with terra cotta-tiled roofs were built in periods of prosperity for wealthy Hydraean families by Italian and Genoese architects, influenced by the Italian architecture of the day. Ships sailed into the harbour laden with furniture, musical instruments, paintings, even music and dance teachers from Europe.

An impressive pair of buildings from that epoch are the harbour master's office (formerly the lazaretto) and the group of dwellings where the foreign teachers lived. Next door is the Municipal Art Gallery and Concert Hall which was until three years ago a powder-magazine! The island's strong maritime tradition lives on in the imposing mansion of the naval hero

A. Tsamados (1774-1825), which housed, in the period following the revolution, part of the School of Merchant Marine Officers.

In the same neighbourhood you will see a few newly-built villas and houses with brightly-painted facades. Two features shared by all these houses are their flowering gardens and large split-level verandas which offer a view of the harbour and the sunset. Atop Kastro hill stand the windmills which once ground the island's grain.

Another sight to see is the Rafalias Pharmacy in the centre of town; established in 1890, it has kept the appearance of an old pharmacy.

In the Kala Pigadia quarter, at the foot of Kiafa hill, see the mansion of the Gorogiannis family from Epirus; it has a traditional Macedonian-style sitting room. In the small square in this quarter are two wells dating from 1800, when the town still used rain-water. Situated in the old

An impressive pair of 18th-century buildings: the harbour master's office and the group of dwellings next to it

Kiafa quarter is the interesting Church of Agios Ioannis Nisteftis with 18th-century frescos, and that of Agios Konstantinos Idreos, built of hewn stone, which celebrates its Saint's Day festival on 14 November. It was built on the foundations of the house where the local saint lived and fell a martyr to the Turks in 1800.

The Metropolis, dedicated to the As-

The imposing Tsamados mansion, which houses part of the School for Merchant Marine Officers (far right), as seen from the upstairs door of the E. Tombazis mansion

The *Gorogiannis mansion at far right* (Stroumboulis collection)

sumption of the Virgin, was built in 1648 and served as a monastery church until 1832. It is a three-aisled domed basilica. In 1769 it was demolished by a major earthquake and completely rebuilt by pious islanders. In its courtyard stand the busts of A. Miaoulis, King George I, A.

The Church of Agios Konstantinos Idreos
The Metropolis in Hydra was so respected by the islanders that no ships left the harbour on the Day of the Assumption of the Virgin. In the background the old Kiafa quarter can be seen.

Lignos and L. Kountouriotis, all works of the Tinian sculptor D. Filipotis (1886). See, too, the cenotaph of L. Kountouriotis (1769-1852) and the marble monument honouring the Greeks who fell in the Balkan Wars. The smaller of its two bell-towers dates from 1806 and the larger from 1874; the latter has a clock and a bell weighing approximately two tons. During the 1821 Revolution, the monastery was a political and cultural centre, and served as a meeting-place for the island's elders.

On the inland road to Kamini, two sights to see are the Old Folks' Home (Theodorakis mansion) and the Kriezis mansion, which originally had a flat roof; its sloping roof is a later addition. It now houses the atelier of the American painter Bruce Marden.

The monastery (Metropolis) cells house the Mayor's Office and a small ecclesiastical museum.

West of the harbour the austere but architecturally impressive two- and three-story sea-captains' mansions are concentrated: One was the home of L. Kountouriotis. A folklore museum in its own right, it has a famous collection of portraits. Another is the Voulgaris mansion. Well

There is more to Hydra than its beaches. The island's interior has much more to offer. Nothing should be passed up hurriedly; every corner of the island is waiting to photographed! The yellow building at upper left is the mansion of L. Kountouriotis.

The great one-eyed sea captain, who made a major contribution to the Revolution, L. Kountouriotis (National Historical Museum)

Interior and courtyard of the G. Kountouriotis mansion (Stroumboulis collection)

worth a visit is the Church of Ipapanti, dating from 1780, with an important carved wooden iconostasis and priceless icons. The island's artistic tradition continues in the department of the School of Fine Arts housed in the old mansion of the naval hero E. Tombazis (1780-1810), on Mili hill. The School bought it in 1936, and it is now being repaired so that it can continue its cultural contribution to Greece. Close by are the mansions of Votsis, Ikonomou (which once had a hall for concerts and dance productions and a reception hall with furnishings imported from Genoa; unfortunately it is no longer in Greek hands). Another mansion is that of G. Kountouriotis (it was bequeathed to Admiral Pavlos Kountouriotis and sold to the Ministry of Culture in 1991). Nearby is the tomb of of P. Kountouriotis. At the base of Mili hill, near the waterfront's western fortress, is a level stretch of high ground from which the view of Dokos and the coast of the Peloponnese is splendid.

In Hydra you can swim off the island's inhospitable shores, within the bounds marked by buoys. The water is deep and crystal-clear. An ideal spot for able swimmers is Spilia (= cave) tou Bariami.

On the coastal road to Kamini stands the Boundouris mansion, which still has its flat roof, as well as certain Renaissance elements.

Hydra gives visitors the opportunity to experience the island's old way of life in a modern environment. Hydraean sea-captains' mansions, decorated in particularly good taste, have been converted into hotels and guesthouses with local colour. (Unfortunately the mansions of the famous sea-captains of the Revolution are not yet open .to the public!) Nestled in splendid gardens are fine restaurants for a variety of tastes and pocketbooks. Small traditional tavernas offer the day's catch accompanied by wine straight from the barrel, and quaint ouzo bars grill octopus over hot coals along the streets. Sample the traditional almond cookies in

Bariami cave is frequented by good swimmers.

Congenial animals outside the Hydra Historical Archives. Donkeys supply transportation in this vehicle-free environment. In Hydra time seems to stand still; island life goes on at a pace inherited from the past.

the old patisseries. In the jewellers' shops, souvenir shops and art galleries you will find hand-made jewellery, knitted garments, ceramics, folk-art items, paintings and icons, and, of course, sponges.

As a centre of the arts, Hydra holds various events, concerts, exhibitions and lectures of all kinds. The last Sunday of the Mardi Gras season is celebrated with a popular carnival, where traditional dances are performed and the wine is on the house. The March 25 national holiday and Easter are also celebrated in splendour. Here the epitaphios procession on

Good Friday is unique in that it winds up in the sea at Megalo Kamini! On Easter Sunday an effigy of Judas is burned amidst a riot of pistol-fire. Between June 21st and 25th, in the framework of Nautical Week, the Miaoulia celebrations are held in honour of Admiral A. Miaoulis; they include sailboat races, swimming events and displays by the Navy's fleet. On August 15, a grand celebration is held at the Metropolis, with companies per-

Mansions of Kountouriotis (upper right), Ikonomou (lower right), Votsis (upper left) and Tombazis (lower left). Agios Athanassios hill and chapel are also visible.

forming local dances. In September the island welcomes the International Marionette Festival, with the participation of famous actors and marionettes from all over the world.

Excursions are organised from the harbour to points around the island, as well as to Porto Heli, Kosta and the ancient theatre in Epidaurus.

On the road to Mandraki stands the new building of the Hydra Historical Archives; it also houses the Historical Museum exhibiting archaeological artefacts,

The developed beach of Miramare in Mandraki

mementoes of the 1821 Revolution and an important art gallery. Unfortunately, the museum remains closed for technical reasons. You can take a boat or walk to Mandraki, where a restored 18th-century shipyard forms part of a luxury hotel. This was the site of the island's naval station during the Revolution. At the developed beach of Miramare, the water is quite deep; water-sports equipment is available to rent.

Hydra - Inland Monasteries

Despite the fact that the name Hydrea bespoke the island's profusion of springs, today it is a rocky, arid and thirsty land. It has, however, many beauty spots to show the visitor to its interior. On foot or on the back of one of Hydra's numerous donkeys, you can visit the historic Monastery of Profitis Ilias on the top of a hill (500 m), with a splendid view out over the harbour. Built in 1815, it has a large library. You can see the cell where the revolutionary hero Theodoros Kolokotronis was among those imprisoned for four months in 1825 by the Kountouriotis government. Close by is the convent of Agia Evpraxia, founded in 1821. The nuns make and sell fine silk embroidery.

Another road runs up from the town to the convent of Agia Matrona dating from 1865, a characteristic example of the island's monastic architecture. On donkeyback you can continue on to the monastery of Agia Triada built in 1704, where only one monk remains. To the east stands the small nunnery of Agios Nikolaos. From there you can go on to Limnioniza Bay, which served from ancient times to the Middle Ages as an observation post looking out on the coast of the Peloponnese.

Eros peak commands a panoramic view of the harbour and the Saronic Gulf in one direction and of the Sea of Myrtoon in another.

You can swim in the Bay of Kasteva. The path to the east winds up at the nunnery of Panagia in Zourva, dedicated to the Birth of the Virgin. It celebrates with a festival on September 8.

At the country chapel of Zoodohos Pigi on difficult-to-reach Cape Zourva, fortified Early Helladic Dryopian grazing land and a port where passing ships took on supplies of water have been discovered.

The Monastery of Agia Evpraxia (Stroumboulis collection)

North of Cape Rigas, on the Bay of Agios Konstantinos around the chapel of the same name, Mycenean and post-Mycenean potsherds were discovered: this was a way-station for ships sailing on to the Cyclades.

Hydra - Kaminia - Vlihos

Caiques sail daily from the harbour to

Unquestionably a jewel of the Aegean, Hydra's capital clings to two rocky hills. (View from the Monastery of Profitis Ilias)

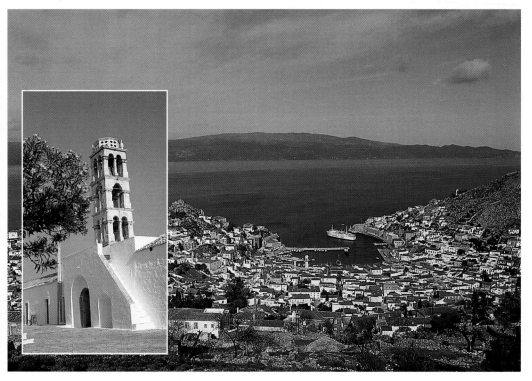

Vlihos beach

Kaminia and Vlihos.

There are two ways of getting to **Kaminia** on foot: Climb the stairs in Navarhou Kriezi Street. You will pass the square building housing Hydra's central market. Then take the torrent bed down to Megalo Kamini. The other way is along the seashore. Setting out to the left of the harbour you will walk along next to the sea. Below the road to Kamini is Avlaki, a small beach with a few trees.

Nowadays this village has expanded to become part of the town. Opposite the little harbour in Megalo Kamini lies the rocky islet of Agios Nikolaos with its chapel of the same name. Megalo Kami-

ni's pebble beach is a nice place for children to bathe.

Here the Epitaphios procession on Good Friday makes a unique detour. The island's young men remove their shoes and socks, roll up their trouser-legs and carry the epitaphios into the sea. They lower it until it touches the water and the priest says a prayer for the sailors out at sea.

A half hour's walk will bring you to the small, picturesque port of **Vlihos**. Its little isolated tavernas and small beach, reddish in colour, a striking contrast to the white houses and Church of Taxiarhis, make quite an unusual picture. The northwest side of the hill of Horiza and the area between it and Vlihos beach, were the site of the island's main settlement in Late Helladic times. At the fortified site of Palamida, where the islanders took refuge after the Methana volcano erupted, scattered fragments of pots from the Hellenistic and Roman eras have been discovered. The medieval bridge on the road to **Molos** – also on the west coast – and the medieval ceramics found in the area are evidence that the region was

Megalo Kamini cove and the rocky islet of Agios Nikolaos with its namesake chapel

Molos beach

never uninhabited. On Molos beach you can swim and find shade under the few pine trees.

An unpaved road from Molos leads to the country homes at **Episkopi**, in a splendid pine forest. The village received its name from the fact that in antiquity this was a lookout post where the sea was surveyed (= episkopo) and a signal sent to the shore of Hermione opposite in case of danger.

The island's main Early Helladic settlement has been identified in this area. Only a few traces of it remain, after the centuries of destruction wrought by a succession of sheep-pens and cultivation of the land. On the rocky eastern edge of the plateau, also known as Episkopi, stood the Mycenean acropolis. A few Mycenean graves, apparently belonging to poor people, were discovered in the area. Also found were Byzantine coins from AD 900-1300, from the Peloponnese.

The little port of Nissiza served Episkopi; there, too, an Early Helladic settle-

Strange rock formations near Cape Bisti

ment was discovered. Quail are hunted in this area in the autumn.

At the small Church of Agios Georgios on Cape Bisti on the southwest coast of the island, an Early Helladic settlement has come to light.

Boats moor in the turquoise Bay of Agios Nikolaos beyond Cape Bisti. Those who do not have their own boat may visit the area by caique. This bay was also used in ancient times as a water supply depot for passing ships.

The chapels of Agios Nikolaos (left) and Agios Georgios (right) on Cape Bisti

Spetses

Name

The place-names of the islands' ancient settlements, dating from a time when there was no national or historical consciousness, not even a mythological tradition, were merely descriptions of each place. Thus Spetses was called *Pityoussa* due to its profusion of pine-trees (pitys = pine-tree). Because Spetses fell into oblivion during the next centuries, it was never renamed for some mythical figure, but retained the same name up to early Byzantine times. In the 6th and 7th centuries, however, Slavic and Arab invasions laid waste to the island and the name Pityoussa was corrupted to *Isola di Spezzie* (= Isle of Spices) by the Venetians and to *Petza* or *Petsa* by the second wave of Arvanite refugees during the 18th century.

Mythology

Myth has it that Pitys was a nymph with whom both the wind-god Boreas and the demon Pan were in love. But because she chose the latter, Boreas whipped her and threw her over a cliff. Gaea, however, mother of the whole world and nurturer of all creatures, took pity on her and changed her into a tree (pitys).

History

The oldest artefacts found to date in the Argosaronic Gulf area were unearthed in Zogeria in Spetses. These were two Mesolithic flint spearheads which probably indicate nothing more than a passing visit by hunters in search of water from the nearby Fraghthi cave on the Argolic Gulf.

The Early Helladic settlements discovered in Spetses and Velopoula (between Spetses and Milos) were used as way-stations between the Peloponnese and the Cyclades. There was also a limited Dryopian presence on the island around the end of the Late Helladic Era (13th century BC). The island's few inhabitants during the centuries that followed are not of any particular historical interest.

Around the end of the Mycenean Era (approximately 1170 BC), Pityoussa was attacked by Myceneans. During the Persian Wars, inhabitants of the island may have participated in the historic Battle of Salamis. During the Peloponnesian War the island may have been attacked by the Athenians.

From the 5th to the 4th century BC the island would appear to have been an extension of the territory (a naval base or grazing land) of the dominion of the city of Halieis. It was attacked by the Macedonian, Demetrius the Besieger, at the same time that he attacked the rulers of the Peloponnese, who were also Macedonians. The city of Halieis was destroyed and as it fell into oblivion, so did Spetses.

In 167 BC, Greece became a Roman province, but repeated pirate invasions left the coastal areas desolate. That was the reason that Strabo did not consider the islands of the Argosaronic Gulf worth mentioning. Many of the inhabitants of Pityoussa must have moved to the safe coastal towns of the Peloponnese, which were protected by the Romans.

When the Byzantine Empire was divided up, Spetses was ceded to the Venetians, who kept it until 1460, when it

Agia Marina beach, drenched in greenery, explains the island's ancient name.

Hatzigiannis Mexis (National Historical Museum)

passed to the Turks. After the fall of the Morea (1461), the island was laid waste by the Turks. Later it was settled by Peloponnesian Arvanite refugees, first on the Bays of Agii Anargiri and Zogeria. The

Figurehead from the Spetsiot ship "Epaminondas", *property of Lazarou or Orloff* (Spetses Museum)

new settlers worked as stock-breeders, but the need to trade in timber from the island's pines prompted them to construct small ships. After Spetses received a second wave of Arvanites in 1540, larger ships took the place of the small ones. And after 1715 the small community which had been established at Kasteli was gradually transformed into a mighty naval power.

The island took part in the Orloff insurrection and raised the Russian flag. As a reprisal, Turks and Albanians set fire to Kasteli in 1770 and many inhabitants were killed or taken prisoner. When the First Russo-Turkish War (1768-1774) ended in the Treaty of Küçük Kaynarca (1774) the prisoners were amnestied; they returned to the island and expanded their town (Kasteli) to the northwest.

The Spetsiot fleet gained the privilege of sailing under the protection of the Russian flag. Spetses was virtually independent, governed by an 8-member council of elders, a local administrator *(bas-kocabassis)* and Turkish representatives appointed by the Spetsiot elders. There followed a second period of economic development brought about chiefly by shipping and commerce; it was given a further impetus by the outbreak of the Napoleonic Wars. The Spetsiots acquired untold wealth. In the years before the Revolution wealthy islanders hired private tutors to teach the Greek language and religion for their children.

Spetses was the first of the Argosaronic islands to participate in the 1821 Revolution. The leader of the Friendly Society of Greek patriots, A. Ipsilantis, named the Spetsiot G. Panou the Society's leader on the island in 1818. When the Revolution broke out, the elders in the Peloponnese wrote to the Spetsiots asking them to join forces in the struggle of the enslaved Greeks. The elders decided at once to take part in the Revolution. On April 3rd, Palm Sunday, the Chancellery (administrative headquarters) was occu-

Bouboulina besieging Nauplion, copied by T. Kontis from a painting by von Hess (1911)

pied without resistance and the island's ships' captains swore their allegiance. The Spetsiots also consulted with the Hydraeans, who agreed to join forces with them.

The Spetsiot fleet (around 55 merchant vessels which had been converted into well-armed men-of-war, with names taken from Greek mythology, conquered fortresses, blockaded the ports of the Aegean, and transported supplies. Valiant Spetsiots also took part in sieges and

The brig "Crimea" of Ioannis G. Kounoupiotis (Spetses Museum)

conquests of towns.

Also of great importance for the Struggle was the firing of the Turkish flagship in the naval battle of September 8th, 1822, because this prevented the Turks from bringing supplies into Nauplio, which then surrendered on November 30th to the Greek besiegers. The women and children were taken to Kamini on Hydra.

The island's merchant fleet continued to prosper until 1845. Later it fell into decline and the population of Spetses dwindled. The island did, however, produce a number of distinguished politicians, admirals, etc., including Alexandros Diomidis, Prime Minister from 1950 to 1951.

Among Spetses' other famous sons in the sphere of the arts and letters, who made great contributions to the cultural evolution of the country, were S. Anargiros, the poets G. Stratigis, G. Pergialitis, G. Logothetis, M. Botassi, the artists E. Altamoura-Boukouri and I. Altamouras, I. Koutsis and D. Litsas.

Detailed English hydrographic map of Spetses, commissioned by Ioannis N. Botassis (Spetses Museum)

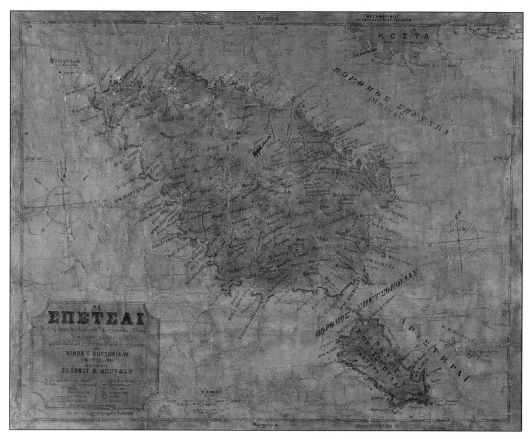

The horses that pull the island's indispensable means of transportation are often photographed, unwitting contributors to the island's picturesqueness.

Spetses Town

Spetses is the last on the string of islands in the Argosaronic Gulf. It has an area of 25.25 square kilometres, a population of 3,427 and lies at a distance of 51 nautical miles from Piraeus.

Spetses town was and still is a grand old lady with historical radiance, aristocratic architecture, a long cultural tradition, physical charm and well-developed tourism.

Pebble mosaics are made up of white and greenish-black pebbles. The technique has been used on the island since AD 700, and has been handed down to successive generations of artisans. In the beginning pebble mosaics served as floors inside houses. Later they came to be used in courtyards, covered entrance-ways, etc. Their construction requires a lot of labour and preparation, including choice of pebbles, patterns and locations. The pebbles are placed in the desired pattern in a lime-based mortar, are tamped down with a heavy wooden mallet, and the gaps are filled in with sand. Pebble mosaics of this type, of particular folkloric interest, may also be encountered in Lindos on Rhodes. (Thimaras collection)

The Hatzianargirou mansion (present-day Koutsis home)

The island is still holding out against a threatened invasion by motor cars, thus assuring both permanent residents and visitors of a special kind of tranquillity, broken only by the roar of an occasional motorcycle. The town is a perfect place for a pleasant walk. Sidewalks, squares and landings between flights of stairs are paved with pebbles, laid out in geometric patterns and marine motifs, e.g. anchors, mermaids, and subjects from ancient, popular and Byzantine tradition. The best way to get around town is in one of the 30 traditional one-horse buggies.

Dapia or **Tapia** (a Turkish name meaning fortified place), the island's most important gun emplacement, served during the Revolution as a meeting-place of the sea-captains; it was also the island's commercial centre. Today it is the hub of tourist goings and comings, as all the roads for touring the town begin from here. This, too, is the starting point for all the excursion boats that sail to other points round the island.

The remarkable mansion of Hatzigiannis Mexis (1754-1844), one of Spetses'

Watching the world go by from one of the Dapia coffee-bars, one acquires a different sense of time.

The Theodorakis Mexis home

most powerful statesmen, and the first governor of the island, now houses the Spetses Museum (open from 8:30 am-4:30 pm daily, closed Mondays). In the courtyard there are two cannons and three busts, one of Hatzigiannis-Mexis, by the Spetsiot sculptor V. Kesses, one of Laskarina Bouboulina and one of the fireship captain Lekas Matrozos.

The ground floor, which remains closed to the public, was used mainly for domestic activities. Two straircas-

The unusual Ginis home, a sophisticated composition of massive blocks

es lead to the first floor, with lavish interior

The Hatzigiannis Mexis mansion, now housing the Spetses Museum, is said to have been built between 1795 and 1798 by Italian master-builders on Arabian and Venetian models.

The Sotirios Anargiros home, the most representative example of a neo-classical mansion.

decoration. Here the museum's three collections, archaeological, historical (mementoes of the Revolution) and folkloric,

are housed. The museum was founded by the professor and academician G. Sotiriou, who carried out excavations on the island. The bones of the local heroine Bouboulina are preserved here. The island's leaders met on the upper floor during the Revolutionary period. King Otho stayed as a guest in this mansion.

Smaller in size is the Theodorakis Mexis home (to the south); it shows some French influence. The Ginis and Kiriazis homes are considered quite original. (The latter is called *Government House* by its owners because they believe it once housed administrative offices.) The N. Kefalonitis home, with lavish interior decoration, belongs to a transitional stage between local architecture and the neoclassical style.

In front of Bouboulina Square with its fine pebble mosaic and the bust of the heroine, to the left of the small park/playground is the Sotirios Anargiros home. This is a superb turn-of-the-century building, showing Egyptian and ancient Greek influence; however it does not harmonise with the rest of the island's architecture.

At the edge of the park is the mansion

Portrait of Bouboulina and a piece of her silk scarf (Bouboulis collection)

of Laskarina Bouboulina, which she inherited from her second husband, D. Bouboulis. It took on its present-day appearance at the beginning of the 19th century. After meticulous, costly repairs and renovations, it now houses the Laskarina Bouboulina Museum (open 8:30 am-3:00 pm, closed Mondays), run by the last descendent of this illustrious family, F. Demertzis-Bouboulis. He will take you on a guided tour of the large pebble-paved courtyard and the inside of the mansion with its lavish decoration, carved Florentine ceiling and a few mementoes of the heroine.

Laskarina Bouboulina, one of Greek history's greatest women, was born on May 12th, 1771 in prison in Constantinople, where her father, the Hydraean Stavrianos Pinotsis, had been incarcerated for participating in the Orloff insurrection, and later died. When her mother married the Spetsiot sea-captain Vassilios Lazarou or Orloff, the family took up permanent residence in Spetses. At the age of 17 Bouboulina married the Spetsiot sea-captain Dimitrios Giannouzas (1788), and when she was 30 she married the Spetsiot sea-captain Dimitrios Bouboulis (1801). Both her husbands were killed in naval battles with Algerian pirates, and Bouboulina found herself a widow with seven children of her own and four stepchildren from Bouboulis' first marriage. She was also heir and executrix of an enormous fortune, which she increased

Exterior of the Bouboulina mansion. Inset: the great hall with its carved Florentine ceiling (Bouboulis collection)

by buying shares in various Spetsiot ships and building three of her own, among them the famous "Agamemnon," the first Greek warship of 1821. She secured the protection of her fortune through a firman of Sultan Mahmud II, and became a member of the Friendly Society. When the Revolution broke out she formed and supported her own army corps, as well as crews for her men-of-war. She brought in weapons and supplies from abroad, which she concealed in secret hiding-places. In this way she slowly exhausted her fortune. She took part in many important naval battles and boosted her troops' morale at difficult moments.

At Haradro near Argos her son Giannouzas fell in battle against 3,000 Turks and Albanians. Her daughter Eleni married the son of Theodoros Kolokotronis, Panos. Bouboulina lived with them in Nauplio until civil war broke out and Panos was murdered and Theodoros im-prisoned. Embittered and on the verge of poverty, she returned to her first husband's mansion in Kounoupitsa.

This illustrious lady came to an inglorious and tragic end when she was murdered on May 22, 1825, during an argument with the Koutsis family, with whose daughter Bouboulina's son Georgios had eloped.

The road to the right of the harbour runs along the waterfront to the Palio Limani. Embrasures with cannon dating from the time of the 1821 Revolution stand witness to the glorious struggles of our ancestors. Here are some of the island's loveliest mansions, protected by law from unseemly alterations. Geometrical austerity, charm and simplicity are the characteristics of Spetsiot homes. Here, as in neighbouring Hydra, they are the work of skilful local traditional master-builders and master-builders from the Peloponnese, Epirus and Italy. Local timber and rough stones were the chief ma-

The Monastery of Agios Nikolaos and the Lighthouse in the Old Harbour

terials used in their construction. Their interiors are long and narrow, reminiscent of the hold of an old sailing-ship. Lofty walls conceal courtyards decked out in greenery and flowers, paved in Dokos stone or pebble mosaics. Essential elements are an exterior stone staircase leading to a pebble-paved landing and a covered door. Most houses are whitewashed on the outside, with terra cotta-tiled roofs and chimneys of many shapes.

The island's post-Byzantine Metropolis, built in 1805 and dedicated to Agios Nikolaos, was once a monastery. See its impressive pebble-mosaic courtyard and the Spetses Heroes' Monument, where the island's sea-captains swore their allegiance to the Revolution. Near Agios Nikolaos is the long, narrow, neo-classical Kapodistrian School (nowadays the Kapodistrian Cultural League) with an important library. Also nearby is the newly-built Church of the Tris Nepmartires Spet-

The Old Harbour quarter. At top left is the Theo-haris home, built of Dokos grey stone

siotes (= Three Latter-Day Spetsiot Martyrs) who died in Hios in 1822. Below the Metropolis is the small beach of Agios Nikolaos.

In a large barrel of rum, the body of Paul Bonaparte, son of Lucian and nephew of Napoleon Bonaparte, was brought to the monastery and kept in one of its cells. He was killed in 1827 when

The Old Harbour: The cannons which had been used as bollards after the Revolution were removed from the sea-floor where they lay under 3 meters of water at a distance of 15-20 meters from each other.

In the island's old ship-yards, metal has not yet su-perseded wood!

The Church of Panagia Armata, where the Revolutionary flag waves

his gun accidentally exploded while he was travelling with the English Admiral Thomas Cochrane (1775-1860) in the Greek flagship of the fleet sailing to Greece to take part in the War of Independence!

Also worth seeing is the Vamvas (Gaitanos) home, incorporating complex elements rare in local architecture. Outstanding among the remaining mansions is the Theoharis (formerly Botsaris) home.

You will come to **Baltiza** or **Palio Li-**

The bell-tower of the Church of the Evangelistria

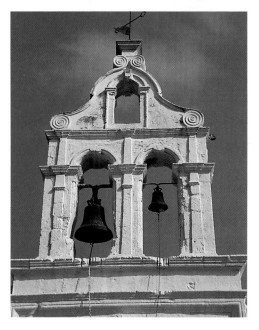

mani (=Old Port), a part of town enclosed by the island's natural harbour, where merchant ships were once built and anchored. Here is the marina where the island's vessels are moored, the old ship-yards, long, narrow buildings with vaulted roofs and small dry-docks where traditional wooden sailing-boats are repaired and maintained. Numerous bars, discos and piano restaurants liven up the old harbour and attest to the island's cosmopolitan reputation.

In this area a fishing village grew up in the Classical Era, the ruins of which were covered by subsequent habitation in the Palio Limani. In fact, Professor Sotiriou, who excavated the early Christian basilica of Evangelistria dating from AD 62, found evidence that it had been built on the ruins of an ancient 4th-century BC temple, perhaps of Poseidon.

In the Evangelistria quarter, see the Anagnostis Botassis home, built in stages in 1798, 1802 and 1808. One of the loveliest rooms in the house is the reception hall (mussafir onda) on the second floor, which is a simulation of the interior of Botassis' ship!

Near Faros stands the Church of Panagia tis Armatas or Armadas, built by the Koutsis family in commemoration of the victory of the Hydraeans, Spetsiots and Psarians over the Turkish/Egyptian fleet on September 8th, 1822 in the strait between Hydra and Spetses. Inside the church is the marvellous painting by Ioannis Koutsis (1887) depicting this naval battle, known as the Battle of the Argolic Gulf or the Battle of Spetses. The last event for those who would like to welcome in the autumn away from Athens is the local festival of Panagia Armata on September 8th. It involves a re-enactment of the historic naval battle. A replica of the Turkish flagship is burned, while fireworks fill the sky. The festivities include athletic events, local dances, etc.

The retreat of the enemy fleet, superior in numbers, on the day of the historic battle is attributed to the courage of Kosmas Barbatsis, that daring man who fired the Turkish flagship on September 8th, an act which essentially decided the outcome of the battle. Also instrumental was the heroism of Hatzigiannis Mexis' and A. Androutsos' 60 men: Watching the Turks approaching, and realising they were outnumbered, Mexis had a stroke of genius. The Spetsiot warriors took off their red fezzes and hung them on some tall bushes with large bunches of red flowers which grew near Faros. So the invaders, not being able to tell from a distance which were fezzes and which were flowers, could not estimate the size of the army!

On Faros promontory is what is known as the *cannon emplacement esplanade*. It is a large park containing cannon emplacements, an anchor of epic proportions and animal sculptures created by

Spetsiots burn the Turkish flagship during the Armata celebrations. (Thimaras collection)

the well-known Spetsiot artist Natalia

Bronze statue of Kosmas Barbatsis, by Natalia Mela

The Church of the Analipsi

Mela out of various pieces of metal and farming implements. Another of her works is the bronze statue of the Spetsiot Revolutionary Kosmas Barbatsis; the statue was financed by the French philhellene Annie Sluberger.

In the **Analipsi** quarter, at the Church of the same name, the islanders keep up the old Easter custom of setting off fireworks. The young people also burn an old boat.

The road to the west of the port of Dapia runs along the waterfront to the Possidonio Hotel, built between 1911 and 1914. Many famous people of that era have been guests here. In the middle of the square stands the bronze statue of Bouboulina, another of Natalia Mela's works.

The **Kounoupitsa** quarter, to the northwest of Spetses town, was founded after the 1821 Revolution. For lovers of quiet places and long walks, this area, with its luxury hotels, little tavernas serv-

The statue of Bouboulina in Possidonio Square

The stately Possidonio Hotel

ing fresh fish and delicious snacks, and seaside bars, is the best place to stay. Some of the island's most beautiful historic homes are in this area, among them Bouboulina's "country" house, where the great Revolutionary heroine lived during the last years of her life. She inherited this stone house with its high garden walls and splendid pebble mosaic from her first husband.

Near Possidonio stands the home of the old Spetsiot industrialist D. Daskalakis; further to the west is the facade of his old spinning-mill, a characteristic example of turn-of-the-century industrial architecture. The present-day Spetses City Hall, formerly the home of N. Kiriakos, eminent sea-captain and Revolutionary fighter, also stands on the Kounoupitsa waterfront; it is one of the last mansions to be built during the great shipping boom of 1795-1815. The square building bears certain Renaissance elements, intimations of neoclassicism. In the Tsalis (Lembessis) home, at the bend in the road, im-

The Boukouris home

portant frescos preserved on the ceilings were probably painted by an Italian artist.

The far end of Kounoupitsa is known as **Souribouti** (Sur-im-but, an Arvanite word for low sand). Houses in this area are smaller. Standing out among them is the home of G. Boukouris, local administrator of the island from 1816 to 1818, with a fine pebble mosaic. Here the great Spetsiot artist Eleni Altamoura-Boukouri

The Kounoupitsa quarter (Kounoupitsa is the Arvanite name for the Chaste-tree).

The Church of the Resurrection in Kounoupitsa

"Scholon" beach. The buildings of the Anargirios and Korgialenios School are visible.

was born, lived out the final years of her life and died.

On the outskirts of town are the buildings of the Anargirios and Korgialenios School of Spetses, once a boarding-school where the scions of aristocratic families from Greece and abroad were sent. Modelled on English boarding schools, it was founded by Sotirios Anargiros, one of the island's great benefactors, and first opened its doors in 1927. Its five massive buildings stand in spa-cious grounds and contain modern laboratories, libraries, a meteorological station, etc. In Spetses Town, the best beach for swimming and water sports is the one near the school, known as *ton Scholon* (= schools).

Sotirios Anargiros, a great visionary of his time, took up permanent residence in Spetses in 1899, when the only visitors were the select guests of the island's wealthy families. He realised at once that

The Kasteli quarter

Among the few pre-Revolutionary buildings still standing in the Kasteli quarter are the Churches of the Assumption, Taxiarhes and Agia Triada.

the island could be developed for tourism, and in 1913 he bought and reforested half the island with pine-trees. He also built the circular road and completed the water system. In 1914 he opened the island's first hotel, the Possidonio.

Near the School is the big Kasteli Hotel (formerly Xenia), where many holidaymakers stay. Next to it on your left, on the pine-clad hills, stands the *Engineers' Quarter*, as the relatively new part of town, **Ligoneri**, is known. It was named Ligoneri (= little water) after a small spring of water that trickles out of the rocky hill. In a small clump of pines, which were miraculously spared in the recent forest-fire, stands the old chapel of Panagia tis Elonas, which celebrates on the Saint's Day of Zoodohos Pigi. Buses link the area with the town.

Southwest of Kounoupitsa on a hill stands the **Kasteli** quarter, which comprised Spetses Town before 1800. About 500 m from the coast, it lies in a rocky, naturally fortified setting, bounded by the Agios Georgios and Kounoupitsa torrents.

According to G. Sotiriou, a farming community grew up here in Classical times. The islanders took refuge here after the devastation caused by the eruption of the Methana volcano, as shown by the scattered potsherds from Hellenistic and Roman times. Traces were also found of a town dating from the 16th cen-

tury AD, and the place-name *Castelli* is mentioned by Venetian authors. During the latter part of the Turkish occupation, Kasteli was inhabited again. By 1715, when it was attacked by the Turks, the town had been fortified with a sturdy wall, formed in part by the outer walls of the houses.

Today's pleasant, picturesque quarter is not at all reminiscent of the 18th-century town, since the wall no longer exists, few of the old houses are still standing, and it now neighbours on newer quarters of town. Kasteli does retain its old churches, which are the only pre-Revolutionary buildings still standing. The area's most important church, which once served as the island's Metropolis, is the Church of the Assumption. The islanders speak with devotion of the miraculous icon of the Virgin which survived almost unscathed the fire set by the Turks after the Orloff insurrection, and about the important but par-

Spetses' tavernas are the right place for lovers of seafood.

tially ruined 17th-century frescos. Other important churches are the Church of the Taxiarhes (1805), the Church of Agia Triada (1793) with a beautiful carved wooden iconostasis, and the Church of Agios Vassilios, built on the town's highest point. Around Agios Vassilios are about 60 ruined windmills and traces of the old wall. A much newer church is Agia Markella, built by a gang of prisoners!

Anargiros' predictions about Spetses were right on the mark, and the foundations he set for tourist development in the early 1900 have endured down to the present: Hotels, hostels, modern guest houses built in the island style of architecture and rooms to rent in private homes welcome the island's many visitors. In the restaurants and tavernas, you may sample the local specialty, *"Fish a la Spetsiota"* (baked in the oven with tomato and garlic). For your entertainment, there are two outdoor cinemas, three discos, and a number of bars and bouzouki music halls (with traditional greek music). Souvenir shops offer jewellery, unusual gifts and examples of popular art.

For getting around on the island, you can rent a motorbike or bicycle. Buses will take you to most of the island's beaches to swim and have a meal. The more inaccessible beaches and the coast of the Peloponnese opposite (Kosta, Porto Heli, Nauplio, Monemvassia, etc.) may be reached by caiques and excursion boats.

Agia Marina beach

Spetses - Agia Marina - Agii Anargiri - Agia Paraskevi

Spetses offers a very wide variety of excursions. On the east coast is the village of **Agia Marina**, with modern villas, tavernas and a developed beach suitable for water sports. The water here is a good place for snorkelling.

The most recent cursory excavations near the country chapel of Agia Marina brought to light 3,000-year-old artefacts. In 1970 the then Curator of Antiquities Dimitrios Theoharis, on a tip from the journalist Adonis K. Kirou, discovered a significant Early Helladic settlement. The dig, unique in the Aegean area and rich in finds, was illuminating, because it gave us information about the Pelasgian settlers and the naval stations they established in the islands of the Argosaronic Gulf. The fact that obsidian from Milos was worked in the area points to links with the Cyclades. The rise in sea-level covered a large portion of the peninsula; this can be seen in the Roman tombs visible on the sea-floor.

Five hundred meters offshore lies the lush green islet of **Spetsopoula** (called *Aristera* in antiquity, and *"Sette Pozzi"* = "seven wells" by the Venetians). It is now the property of Spetses' present-day benefactor, the shipowner Stavros Niarhos. Caiques make the round of Spetsopoula. A farming community grew up here in the 5th-4th centuries BC.

To the southwest of Spetses Town is the convent of Agii Pantes, with 40 nuns. It was built in the early 1800s on the site of a wayside chapel of the same name, and commands a marvellous view of Hydra, Trikeri, Dokos and Hermione. Nearby St. Nektarios of Aegina lived for a short time as a hermit. Facing it on the hills opposite, the island's Orthodox adherents of the Julian calendar built another monastery dedicated to Panagia Gorgoepikoos, whose buildings are in no way inferior in magnificence.

The magnificent Monastery of Agii Pantes and the newer one of the adherents to the Julian calendar.

Unlike Spetses town, the rest of the island is profusely vegetated, with pine forests reaching right down to the coast. Excursion buses from Spetses Town stop at small idyllic beaches on their way to the stunningly beautiful inlet of Xilokeriza, where the water is turquoise blue. Its developed beach and small snack-bar attract many of the island's holiday-makers.

The buses wind up in the constantly

The beach of Xilokeriza, once lush and green

growing resort of **Agii Anargiri**, with its restored churches of Pano and Kato Agii Anargiri, a hotel, a developed beach with schools of water-skiing and wind-surfing, and restaurants offering Greek music. Turtle-doves and quail are hunted in this area. On the fortified hill where the small Church of Pano Agii Anargiri stands, traces of a Mycenean settlement have been unearthed. Ask one of the locals to show you the small Cave of Bekiris (50 m to the right of the beach), which served as a hiding-place for the Spetsiots during the Orloff insurrection.

You can reach the pebble beach of Agia Paraskevi, with a snack-bar, by road or by caique. On July 26, its namesake Church holds a traditional festival. The small pine woods here is a good place for a picnic. Near the Church traces of an Early Helladic settlement were discovered.

Spetses - Zogeria - Profitis Ilias

By caique you can sail to the pine-clad beaches of Vrelou and Zogeria farther to the west.

The inlet at Zogeria is the twin of the one near the chapel of Agios Georgios. The beach is developed; try the delicious specialty of its small taverna, chicken and spaghetti.

On the northern point of Zogeria Bay, obsidian flakes were discovered. This area, like Agia Marina, seems to have been a way-station between the Cyclades and the Argolid during the Bronze Age. Both were abandoned for unknown reasons late in the 3rd millennium BC. Also discovered here were Athenian coins, near a tower built by the Athenians where fires were lit to send signals to the acropolis at Halieis. Coins from the 5th-century AD Byzantine settlement have also come to light. Offshore lies the rocky islet of Bourboulo or Karavofanaro, much esteemed by fishermen.

An unpaved road runs from Vrellos through Spetses' pine forest up to Profitis Ilias (285 m) and the chapel of Panagia

Agii Anargiri beach

Agia Paraskevi beach. On the right is the Church of the same name.

tou Daskalaki on the summit of the moun-tain. Near the chapel is a hunters' refuge and a newly-built observation post for for-est fire prevention.

The beach at Zogeria

Bibliography

ANTONIADOU, EKATERINI – BOUBOULIS-DEMERTZIS, FILIPOS: *"Spetses, Historical Retrospection"*, a publication of the Society "Bouboulina" of Cultural Services, Spetses, 1992.

BOUBOULIS-DEMERTZIS, FILIPOS: *"Laskarina Bouboulina"*, a publication of the "Bouboulina" Society of Cultural Services, Spetses, 1992.

* FILINTRA, MARIANNA: *"Spetses, Traditional Greek Architecture"*, Melissa Editions, Athens, 1985.

FOTIADIS, DIMITRIS: *"The 1821 Revolution"*, Melissa Editions, Athens, 1971-1972.

GITAKOS, MICHAEL: *"The Faneromeni Monastery of Salamina, from a Historical and Hagiographic Viewpoint"*, a publication of the Holy Metropolis of Megara and Salamina, Athens, 1993.

* KIRIAKOPOULOS, KOSTAS: *"Poros – Trizina"*, "Calauria" – K. Kiriakopoulos Editions, second edition, Athens, 1994.

KIROU, ADONIS: *"At the Crossroads of the Argosaronic"*, Volume I, Historical and Archaeological Travelogue in an Area of the Aegean Sea, Athens, 1990.

KOULIKOURDI, GEORGIA P.: *"Aigina, Greece"*, a publication of the Eparchy of Aigina.

KOULIKOURDI, GEORGIA P. – ALEXIOU, SPIROS N.: *"Aigina, a Guide to its History and Monuments"*, 1952.

KREMASIOTIS, THEODOROS D.: *"Our Hydra"*, Athens, 1992.

* LEOUSSIS, STELIOS: *"Aigina, 35 Centuries of Civilisation"*, Aeacus Tourist Editions, Athens.

* MAVRELI, M.D.: *"Aigina, Poros, Hydra, a One-Day Cruise"*, Hellenic Travel Press – Mavreli Editions, Athens, 1992.

* NEUHOF, SONIA: *"Aigina"*, E. Tzaferis Editions A.E. – Apollo, 1978.

PALLAS, D.: *"Archaeological Points on Salamina"*, Archaeological Bulletin 42 (1987), studies, pp. 169-227.

PAPADOPOULOU, MEROPI: *"Tribute to Aigina"*, Ikones magazine, July, 1993.

PAPADOPOULOU, MEROPI: *"Tribute to Hydra"*, Ikones magazine, August, 1993.

PAPATHANASSI-MOUSSIOPOULOU, K.: *"Traditional Manifestations of our People"*, Pitsilos Editions, Athens, 1992.

* ROSSITER, STUART: *"Blue Guide"*, Ernest Benn Ltd., Great Britain, 1980.

ROUMANI, IOANNA: *"The Monastery of Poros"*, D. Mavromatis – Holy Monastery of Zoodohos Pigi of Poros Editions, Poros, 1992.

SPIROU, GEORGIOS: *"Salamina, Then and Now"*, Georgios Spiros Editions.

* Tourist Guide: *"This Summer in Hydra"*, Giannis Kiritsakis, publisher, Athens, 1988.

* Tourist Guide: *"Welcome to Poros – Hydra – Ermioni – Spetses – Porto Heli"*, Vassilis Giannakis, publisher, Athens 1993.

* Tourist Guide: *"Where to Go – What to See in Poros"*, Infografic Studio Editions, Athens, 1990.

"Kathimerini" daily newspaper: *"Tribute to Hydra"*, Sunday, September 1994.

* *Exists in English translation*

How to Get there

• You can get to Salamina on one of the frequent ferries from Perama (tel. 44.13.178), either on the Perama-Paloukia route or the Perama Megarida-Faneromeni route.
You can reach the rest of the islands of the Argosaronic on one of the ferries sailing from Piraeus (Harbour Master's Office telephone No. 41.24.585). During the winter they take the route Aegina-Methana-Poros-Hydra or Aegina-Methana-Poros-Hydra-Spetses. In the summer sailings are more frequent and routes vary according to the requirements of the season.
Ferries and caiques connect Poros and Galatas round the clock (Galatas Harbour Master's Office telephone No. 0298-22.274)
• Flying Dolphins sail from the port of Piraeus (central Flying Dolphin agency 42.80.001), taking the following routes:
Piraeus to Aegina; Piraeus to Hermione, calling at Aegina, Methana, Poros and Hydra; Piraeus to Hermione, calling at Poros and Hydra; Piraeus to Porto Heli, calling at Poros, Hydra and Spetses; Piraeus to Porto Heli, calling at Hydra and Spetses. In winter, the only route taken is Piraeus-Methana-Poros-Hydra.
Flying Dolphins from Zea Marina in Piraeus sail to Hydra, via Aegina, Methana and Poros, and to Spetses, via Aegina, Methana, Poros and Hydra.
From the port of Piraeus there is also frequent Flying Dolphin service to Salamina (tel. 41.81.333).
• Methana and Galatas may be reached by buses operating out of the KTEL for the Peloponnese in Kifissou St. (tel. 51.34.588) to Nauplio (Nauplio KTEL 0752-27.323). From there other buses run to Methana via Galatas.
• Linking the islands to each other are motor caiques; excursions are organised by travel agencies. There are also such links to the Peloponnese.
• There is also daily service between Aegina and Angistri.

Useful Telephone Numbers

Salamina:		
	Municipality	46.51.138
	Police and Tourist Police	46.51.100
	Harbour Master's Office	46.53.252/46.51.130
	Health Centre	46.53.555/46.50.808
	Archaeological Museum	46.53.572
	Folklore Museum	46.57.361
	Ferries	46.53.394/46.50.075
	Flying Dolphin Agency	48.20.160/41.81.333
Aegina:		
	City Hall	0297- 22.220
	Police	22.100
	Tourist Police	23.333/22.260
	Harbour Master's Office	22.328
	Hospital	22.209/22.251
	Health Centre	22.222
	Bus Station	22.787
	Taxi Stand	22.635
	Flying Dolphin Agency	24.456/24.571/26.154
	Tourist Information	25.690/23.613

Angistri:	Commune	0297- 91.260
	Police	91.201
	Aegina Harbour Master's Office	22.328
	Hospital	91.215
Methana:	City Hall	0298- 92.324
	Police	92.370
	Tourist Police	92.463
	Rural Clinic	92.332
	Pharmacy	92.839/92.478
	Vromolimni Hot Springs	92.244
	Agios Nikolaos Hot Springs	92.394
	Harbour Master's Office	92.279
	KTEL Inter-City Bus Office	92.340
	Flying Dolphin Agency	92.460
Poros:	Municipality	0298- 22.250
	Galatas Commune	22.411
	Tourist Police	22.256
	Harbour Master's Office	22.274
	P.I.K.P.A. medical station	22.600
	Galatas Health Centre	22.222
	Archaeological Museum	23.276
	Library	25.936
	Flying Dolphin Agency	22.297/22.977
	KTEL Inter-City Bus Office for Galatas	22.480
	Poros Taxi Stand	23.003
	Galatas Taxi Stand	22.321
Hydra:	City Hall	0298- 53.003/52.210
	Police and Tourist Police	52.205
	Harbour Master's Office	52.279
	Hospital	52.181/53.150-1
	Rural Clinic	52.420
	Pharmacy	52.059
	Flying Dolphin Agency	52.019-53.384
Spetses:	City Hall	0298- 72.225
	Police and Tourist Police	73.100
	Harbour Master's Office	72.245
	Hospital	72.472
	Historical Archives	72.994
	Library	72.225
	Flying Dolphin Agency	73.141-2
	Water Taxis	72.072

List of Hotels

Salamina:	AKROGIALI•	Selinia	46.53.341

VOTSALAKIA•	Selinia		46.53.494
PANORAMA•	Moulki		46.62.354
GAVRIIL•	Moulki		46.62.275

Aegina:

EYINITIKO ARHONDIKO•	Aegina	A	0297-24.156/24.968
ATHINA PAVLOU•	Aegina	D	23.091
ARETI•	Aegina	C	22.806
ARTEMIS•	Aegina	D	22.523/25.195
AVRA•	Aegina	C	22.303/25.036
BROWN•	Aegina	C	22.271/25.838
DANAI•	Aegina	B	22.424-5
KLONOS•	Aegina	C	22.640/22.597
MARAS•••	Aegina	A	26.421
MARMARINOS•	Aegina	D	23.510
MIRANDA•	Aegina	D	22.266
NAVSIKA••••	Aegina	B	22.333
NERINA•••	Aegina	B	23.038
PAVLOU•••	Aegina	B	22.795
PEPPAS•	Aegina	E	23.973/25.851
PETRINO SPITI•••	Aegina	C	23838/86.42.031
PLAZA•	Aegina	E	25.600
TOCHIA•	Aegina	E	22.806
PHAROS•	Aegina	C	24.242
ULRIKA•	Aegina	E	22.910/25.600
AEGINA MARIS•	Perdika	B	25.130-1
MOONDY BAY••••	Perdika	B	25.147/61.146-7
HIPPOCAMBUS•	Perdika	D	61.363/61.459
ATHINA•	Souvala		53.060
ALKYONA••••	Souvala	D	53.155
EFI•	Souvala	C	52.214
GALAXY••••	Souvala	C	52.944
XANTHIPPI••••	Souvala	C	52.201/52.606
SARONIKOS•	Souvala	D	52.224
CHRISSI AKTI••••	Souvala	C	52.786/52.881
AIGLI•••	Agia Marina	C	32.221
AKTI•	Agia Marina	C	32.249/32.288
ALONES••••	Agia Marina	C	32.176/32.004
AMMOUDIA•	Agia Marina	C	32.313/32.204
ANTHI•	Agia Marina	E	32.565
ANGELA•	Agia Marina	E	32.556
APOLLON•	Agia Marina	B	32.271/4
ARGO•	Agia Marina	B	32.266/32.471-2
APHAIA•	Agia Marina	C	32.227
BLUE FOUNTAIN•	Agia Marina	A	32.052
BLUE HORIZON•	Agia Marina	C	32.303
GALINI•	Agia Marina	C	32.203

CAROUSSEL•	Agia Marina	C	32.496
DIMITRA••••	Agia Marina	C	32.224
DELFINI•	Agia Marina	E	32.451
HERMES•	Agia Marina	C	32.411
ISSIDORA•	Agia Marina	C	32.414
KAVOS•	Agia Marina	D	32.338
KALLIOPI•	Agia Marina	C	32.225
KARRAS•	Agia Marina	C	32.464
KARIATIDES•	Agia Marina	C	32.331
KLEOPATRA•	Agia Marina	C	32.038
KRONION•	Agia Marina	D	32.495
KYRIAKAKIS•	Agia Marina	C	32.538
LENIA••••	Agia Marina	C	32.315
LOUSSI••••	Agia Marina	C	32.378
LIBERTY•	Agia Marina	C	32.353
MAGDA•	Agia Marina	C	32.325
MARIANA••••	Agia Marina	C	32.336
MARINA•	Agia Marina	C	32.301
BAKOMITROS•	Agia Marina	E	32.441
NEKTARIOS•	Agia Marina	C	32.438
OASIS•	Agia Marina	C	32.312
PANORAMA•	Agia Marina	C	32.202/32.144
POSEIDON•	Agia Marina	C	32.392
PANTELAROS•	Agia Marina	C	32.431-2
SANDY BEACH•	Agia Marina	C	32.149
SARONIS•	Agia Marina	C	32.386
TA TRIA ADELFIA	Agia Marina	C	32.229
PHILIPPOS••••	Agia Marina	C	32.238
HARLEPAS•	Agia Marina	B	32.205
XENI•	Vagia	C	52.435
VAYA•	Vagia	E	52.510
CHRYSSI AKTI••••	Vathy		52.786
SISSY•	Marathonas	D	26.222
ABATIS•	Angistri	C	0297-91.377-8
ANGISTRI•	Angistri	E	91.228
AKTEON•	Angistri	E	91.222
AKTI•	Angistri	E	91.232
ALEXANDRA•	Angistri	E	91.251
ANAGENNISSIS•	Angistri	E	91.332
ANASTASSIOU•	Angistri	E	91.317
ANDREAS•	Angistri	D	91.346
ARTEMIS•	Angistri	E	91.309
GALINI•	Angistri	D	91.219
YANNA•	Angistri	E	91.356
MANARAS•	Angistri	D	91.312
MYLOS•	Angistri	D	91.241

Angistri:

MARY•	Angistri	E	91.421
DINA•	Angistri	D	91.235
NONDAS•	Angistri	E	91.212
PAGONA•	Angistri	E	91.327
POULAKIS•	Angistri	E	91.353
SARONIS•	Angistri	D	91.394
SPASTIRAS••••	Angistri	C	91.218
FLISVOS•	Angistri	E	91.264

Methana:

AITHRA•	Methana	D	0298-92.420
AKTI•	Methana	D	92.387
AMERICAN•	Methana	C	92.285
AVRA•	Methana	B	92.550
DIMA•	Methana	C	92.253
METHANIO•	Methana	C	92.227
PIGE•	Methana	B	92.258
SARONIS•	Methana	B	92.312
STUDIOS HELENA••••	Methana	C	92.227

Poros:

AKTEON•	Poros	C	0298-22.281
ALIKI BEACH•	Poros		25.305/24.264
ALEXOPOULOU•	Poros		22.697
ANDONIOU•	Poros		22.074
VARVERIS•••	Poros		22.227
DIMITRA•	Poros	E	22.697
DIONYSSOS•	Poros	B	24.503
DOUZINAS•	Poros		24.502
HELEN••••	Poros	C	22.501
THEANO•••	Poros	B	22.576
IOANNIDI•	Poros		24.541
KAIKAS•	Poros	B	24.566
LATSI•	Poros	B	22.392
MANESSIS•	Poros	C	22.273
POROS•	Poros	B	22.216-7
POSIDONION••••	Poros	C	22.770
RO••••	Poros	C	24.065
SARON•	Poros	B	22.279
ANGIRA•	Neorio	C	22.368
PAVLOU•	Neorio	B	22.734-6
ANDREADAKIS•	Askeli		24.589
ANIFANDAKIS•	Askeli		22.555
GALAXIAS•	Askeli		24.779
NEA AIGLI•	Askeli	B	22.372
PARASKEVA•	Askeli		24.246
HADZIPERIS•	Askeli		22.034
CHRISSI AVYI•	Askeli		22.277
SIRINA•	Monastiri	B	22.741

GALATIA•	Galatas		0298-22.227
PAPASSOTIRIOU•	Galatas		22.841-2
MANOS•••	Galatas		22.000/23.456
SARONIS•	Galatas		22.356
STELLA MARIS•	Galatas		22.562

Hydra:

ANGELIKA•••	Hydra	C	0298-53.202
AMARYLLIS•••	Hydra	B	52.249
ANDONIOS KOFITSAS•••	Hydra	A	53.227
ARGO•	Hydra	D	52.452
ARIS•	Hydra		53.002/53.811
VOTSIS•	Hydra	A	52.066
GAVALAS••	Hydra	B	52.101
GARDALINOU••	Hydra	B	52.114
GREKO•••	Hydra	B	53.200
GRAFOU••	Hydra	B	52.732
DELFINI•	Hydra	B	52.082
EROFILI•••	Hydra		52.272
THEODOROS•••	Hydra		52.810
IPPOKAMBOS•	Hydra		53.453
KAVALIEROU••	Hydra	B	53.066
KAMINI•••	Hydra	B	52.335
KEHAGIOGLOU••	Hydra	B	52.259
KOUKOUDAKI••	Hydra	B	52.615
KRIEZIS••	Hydra	B	52.424
LITO•	Hydra	C	52.280
MAVROMATIS••	Hydra	B	52.911
MIRANDA•••	Hydra	A	52.230/53.510
MISTRAL•••	Hydra	B	52.509/53.411
BOUAGA•••	Hydra		52.869
BOUNDOURIS••	Hydra		52.845
MORIATOU••	Hydra	B	52.371
NEFELI•	Hydra		53.297
NIKOLOUDI••	Hydra	A	52.344
ORLOFF•••	Hydra	B	52.564/52.495
PAPOUTSI••	Hydra	B	53.038
PARASKEVOPOULOS••	Hydra	B	52.853
PARISSI••	Hydra	B	52.856
PETROCHILOU••	Hydra	B	53.253
RETITANGOS•••	Hydra		53.568
SARANDOPOULOS••	Hydra	A	52.272
SOFIA•	Hydra	D	52.313
SOURELIS••	Hydra	A	52.997
SIDRA•••	Hydra	B	53.401
HYDRA•	Hydra	C	52.102
YDRIZA•••	Hydra	B	52.349
YDROUSSA (ex. XENIA)•	Hydra	B	52.400
HALKIDI••	Hydra	A	53.024
MIRAMARE•••	Mandraki	A	52.300-1

Spetses:	ALEXANDRI•	Spetses	E	0298-73.073
	ANNA-MARIA•	Spetses	E	73.035-6
	ARGO•	Spetses	E	73.225
	ACROPOL•	Spetses	D	72.219
	VILLA ANESSIS•••	Spetses	B	72.474
	VILLA MARTHA•••	Spetses	B	72.147
	VILLA CHRISTINA•••	Spetses	B	72.218/74.228
	ILIOS•	Spetses	C	72.488/72.268
	KAMELIA•	Spetses	E	72.415/73.335
	KASTELI•	Spetses	A	72.311-3
	KLIMIS•	Spetses	D	73.777/73.725
	KOSTA••••	Spetses	B	73.814/73.832
	MYRTOON•	Spetses	C	72.555-6
	POSSIDONION•	Spetses	A	72.308/72.006
	ROUMANIS•	Spetses	B	72.244/72.344
	SPETSES•	Spetses	A	72.602-4
	STELIOS•	Spetses	D	72.364/72.971
	STAR•	Spetses	C	72.214/72.462
	PHAROS•	Spetses	C	72.613-4
	SARANDOS•	Agia Marina	E	73.887
	AKROGIALI•••	Agii Anaryiri		73.695

• Hotel
•• Furnished Rooms
••• Guest House
•••• Furnished Apartments

Index

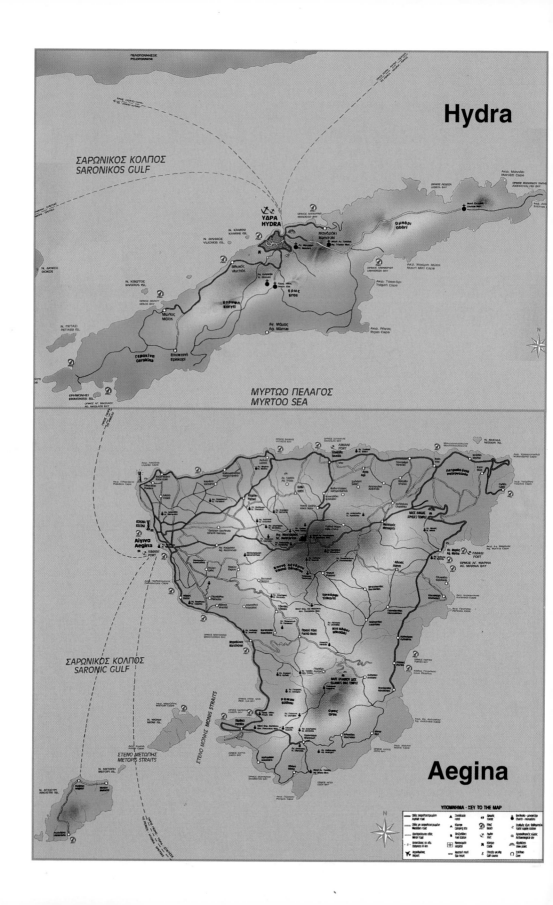

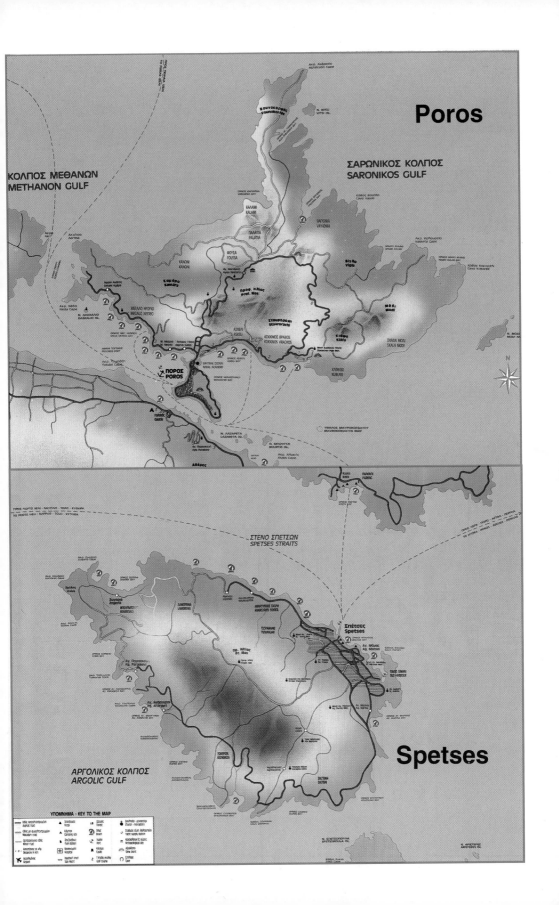

Poros

ΚΟΛΠΟΣ ΜΕΘΑΝΩΝ
METHANON GULF

ΣΑΡΩΝΙΚΟΣ ΚΟΛΠΟΣ
SARONIKOS GULF

ΠΟΡΟΣ
POROS

Spetses

ΣΤΕΝΟ ΣΠΕΤΣΩΝ
SPETSES STRAITS

Σπέτσες
Spetses

ΑΡΓΟΛΙΚΟΣ ΚΟΛΠΟΣ
ARGOLIC GULF

ΥΠΟΜΝΗΜΑ - KEY TO THE MAP

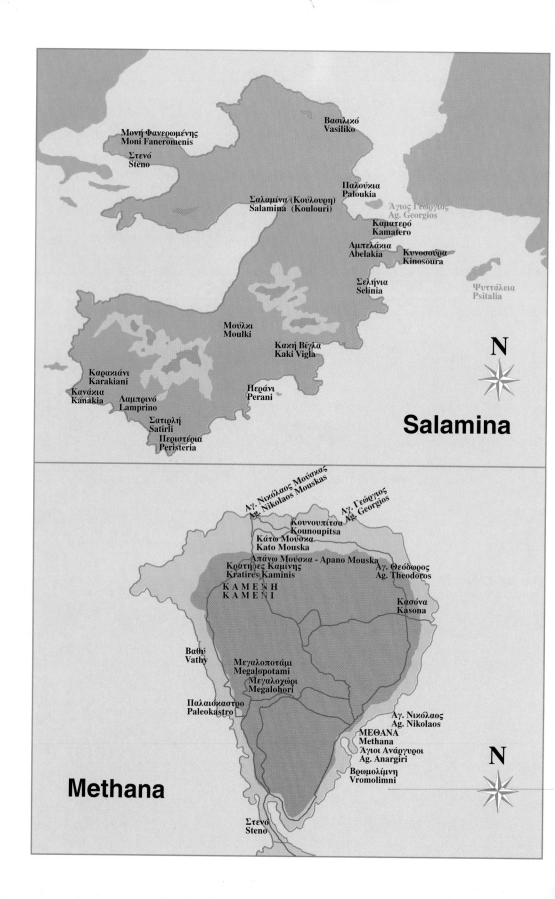

Μονή Φανερωμένης
Moni Faneromenis

Στενό
Steno

Βασιλικό
Vasiliko

Παλούκια
Paloukia

Σαλαμίνα (Κούλουρη)
Salamina (Koulouri)

Άγιος Γεώργιος
Ag. Georgios

Καματερό
Kamatero

Αμπελάκια
Abelakia

Κυνοσούρα
Kinosoura

Σελήνια
Selinia

Ψυττάλεια
Psitalia

Μούλκι
Moulki

Κακή Βίγλα
Kaki Vigla

Καρακιάνι
Karakiani

Κανάκια
Kanakia

Λαμπρινό
Lamprino

Περάνι
Perani

Σατιρλή
Satirli

Περιστέρια
Peristeria

N

Salamina

Αγ. Νικόλαος Μούσκας
Ag. Nikolaos Mouskas

Αγ. Γεώργιος
Ag. Georgios

Κουνουπίτσα
Kounoupitsa

Κάτω Μούσκα
Kato Mouska

Απάνω Μούσκα - Apano Mouska

Κρατήρες Καμίνης
Kratires Kaminis

Αγ. Θεόδωρος
Ag. Theodoros

ΚΑΜΕΝΗ
KAMENI

Κασόνα
Kasona

Βαθύ
Vathy

Μεγαλοποτάμι
Megalopotami

Μεγαλοχώρι
Megalohori

Παλαιόκαστρο
Paleokastro

Αγ. Νικόλαος
Ag. Nikolaos

ΜΕΘΑΝΑ
Methana

Άγιοι Ανάργυροι
Ag. Anargiri

Βρωμολίμνη
Vromolimni

Methana

N

Στενό
Steno